Feminist Theories
and Education
PRIMER

PETER LANG
New York • Washington, D.C./Baltimore • Bern
Frankfurt am Main • Berlin • Brussels • Vienna • Oxford

Leila E. Villaverde

Feminist Theories and Education
PRIMER

PETER LANG
New York • Washington, D.C./Baltimore • Bern
Frankfurt am Main • Berlin • Brussels • Vienna • Oxford

Library of Congress Cataloging-in-Publication Data

Villaverde, Leila E.
Feminist theories and education primer / Leila E. Villaverde.
p. cm.— (Peter Lang primers)
Includes bibliographical references.
1. Feminism and education. I. Title.
LC197.V55   305.4201—dc22   2007032739
ISBN 978-0-8204-7147-1

Bibliographic information published by **Die Deutsche Bibliothek**.
Die Deutsche Bibliothek lists this publication in the "Deutsche
Nationalbibliografie"; detailed bibliographic data is available
on the Internet at http://dnb.ddb.de/.

Cover design by Clear Point Designs

The paper in this book meets the guidelines for permanence and durability
of the Committee on Production Guidelines for Book Longevity
of the Council of Library Resources.

Contents

CHAPTER 1

Introduction

Feminist theory is an academic discipline, an area of study, and feminism is a collective/social movement making us aware of gender, its privilege and inequity. Both feminist theory and feminism are often regarded as singular, monolithic entities that mean one thing, stand for one thing, and speak to one group: women. It is time to widen the lens and understand why, as a society, we focus on dichotomies (black and white, female and male, queer and straight, etc.) while ignoring the continuum of race/ethnicity, gender, sexual identity, class, culture, language, and so on. We tend to seek rather simple explanations for complex phenomena without truly studying the forces that produce these conditions. The reality is that inequity, injustice, and discrimination exist because we continue to blur and obscure what produces them: power (and who wields it). A person, group, or ideology maneuvers power, and unless we discuss how power and its owner(s) are affected by the success or failure of its operation, social conditions cannot change effectively. To com-

prehend a phenomenon or condition fully, we also have to understand what it is not and what external forces or contexts define its identity.

For some, feminism has become the unspoken language of their actions; for others, it is glossed over by capitalist empowerment; and for yet others, it is a historical place or space that informs and forges new spaces for greater analysis in postmodern studies, identity representation, power, and access. A hybrid feminist theory grapples with the continuum of gender identification and expression. It speaks to where we are politically, even though academically some might not have arrived. Despite and in spite, many still ask, "What is feminism?" "Haven't things changed, aren't women in high-powered positions across society (government, business, media/Hollywood), aren't things equal, since women can do just about whatever they want now?" The perception of equality or achievement is not the overwhelming reality. The exception is never the rule, and many young women and men are left shortchanged both by an educational system that ill prepares them for a critical literacy of **agency** and by a society that conflates money with accomplishment.

Agency
an individual's ability to self-advocate and critically negotiate complex power relations

Social circumstances have changed; various career options are available, in contrast to previous limited opportunities for women. These changes are accompanied by new sociopolitical dilemmas and shifts in cultural expectations and priorities, making the argument to refocus on the development of feminist/gender studies literacy one that encompasses identity politics beyond feminism (including queer theory, transnational studies, postcolonial theory, post-structural theory, and critical theory). Simultaneously, we must be skeptical or at least suspicious of so-called "good knowledge" leading to good behavior (Britzman, 1998). We can spend countless hours perfecting language or expanding it, but if we do not spend countless other hours in the struggle of and for education or pedagogy in all its forms and sites (both traditional and nontraditional learning spaces), and, specifically, the devel-

opment of multiple ways of integrating feminist (post-structural—see Chapter Five) critical pedagogy into daily living, it will continue to support and be complicit in a larger system of inequity impenetrable by you or me.

Imagine a young woman who has recently graduated from college with a double major in computer science and women's and gender studies. She has accepted a position as a programmer for a team working on educational software. She has one woman coworker; the rest of her team consists of men. She feels competent and excited to negotiate the politics of the job, yet she finds that time and time again the burden of understanding, negotiating, and dealing with these politics is on her, not her colleagues. Many times she wonders how to initiate change if she is the only one who understands the inequities she witnesses, from the treatment of coworkers to the language used to discuss consumers or clients, to how education or literacy are defined, to the larger social contributions of the software.

Imagine a young man who seeks to find his place yet is challenged by seemingly competing definitions of masculinity and femininity. He has not attended any formal courses on feminism or gender studies but has great access to resources and knowledge at home. Desirous to be popular with friends and love interests, he by default strives to fit in, to perform the stereotype of strength, valor, courage, and disinterest. Nothing fits, everything seems alien, and language escapes him as he struggles to react instead of critique. He hyper-focuses on what the media and his peers perceive as important, such as body image, lackluster brain power, and increased superficial humor. Without the valorized space to reflect through meaningful questions and self-responsibility, he often turns the lack of possibility inward as incapacity and sadness.

These examples illustrate that there are no guarantees in knowing alone and that felt discomfort by itself does not necessarily provide motivation to seek knowledge. Education in itself will not change the

conditions of the workplace, home, relationships, or self. Discomfort by itself will not produce the impetus to seek answers or help one recognize what questions to ask. Knowing needs to be accompanied by multiple actions, specific to context but nonetheless potentially transformative or subversive. Questioning needs to be followed by a consistent sequence of events that encourage further inquiry without involving higher costs. It is imperative for this young woman to find ways to change her environment and the way her company does business, so to speak, without compromising what she knows and how she knows it. Without the skills to negotiate such terrains, her knowledge may easily turn into anger or frustration. Instead of her existing knowledge continuously evolving, it may regress to times where she did not have such fluency with these critical perspectives. Instead of this young woman being a catalyst in changing what this company can do, the company may slowly change her. It is very difficult to maintain our sense of self in the politically charged contexts we enter and negotiate daily, but the primary element is the negotiation; nothing is or needs to be static. Change takes time, research, and vision, particularly change that involves shifts in consciousness and traditions.

For the young man it is equally important to reside in spaces where he is able to relax and not incur further costs to who he is or who he could become so that relationships are perceived not as antagonisms but as coalitions. If not, his sadness and feelings of incapacity will confirm the stoic defense persona of which he has had a short experience. Both scenarios can quickly pivot from incredible potential to status quo. We would hope for more positive youth development and a simultaneous shift of the tectonic plates of gender binaries and roles. My point here is that hope is insufficient and mostly a passive endeavor; we need to be proactive in developing what Anzaldúa (1999) calls **mestiza consciousness** and Sandoval (1991) terms **differential consciousness** (discussed later in this chapter). This is possible only by delving into

Differential consciousness

Chela Sandoval's term for consciousness (method) that allows movement between and among ideological and identity positions, requiring reading power manifestations and using whatever ideology is necessary for resistance

Mestiza consciousness

Gloria Anzaldúa's term for the embodiment of developing a tolerance for contradictions and ambiguity produced by complex identity politics and heritage, living at the crossroads of multiple realities

the rich intersections of multiple theories and practices or lived experiences.

Eaton (2003) states, "Theories become the strategy for change," ways to reimagine the world as we know it, ways to understand the same world, to analyze how it was constructed, how we are constructed, and how we construct it (p. 32). The superimposed gap between theory and practice can be made obsolete by stressing the necessity of both elements to personal and social upheavals. Theory requires active interpretation and ownership by the reader, so that knowledge is converted into strategies for **praxis.** Another way to identify theory is as an intricate conversation with the self and with others, where we think deeply about broader contexts no matter what instigated the inquiry (whether it was a personal issue or a social one). These deep conversations throughout history and culture or across political borders afford new methods for understanding not only ourselves but others around us. Our renewed relationship to theory allows us to accept the responsibility of learning and educating at every turn, not solely in publicly designated spaces for pedagogy. The work undertaken here underscores the importance of creating a **"rhizome"** of ideas and actions that have contributed to and will further feminist theory (in its broadest sense). It is in this way that the door to cross-disciplinary analysis has been forced open (see Chapter Four). In what follows, I bring together several feminist authors who delineate multiple perspectives in feminism and theory to spur our own praxis.

Allison Jaggar (1983) presents a typology of feminist politics and epistemology outlining liberal feminism, traditional Marxism, radical feminism, and socialist feminism. Recognizing there are many ways to be a feminist and the general objections to women's oppression, Jaggar proceeds to distinguish between ideology and political standpoint. She defines liberal feminism as

> resting on a conception of human nature that is radically individualistic . . . believing that women are oppressed insofar as they suffer unjust dis-

Praxis

a spiral in which critical reflection and action continuously inform each other in the service of individual and personal transformation, central to liberatory education

Rhizome

a root; used here as a metaphor for a network of connections between concepts and entities

crimination . . . relying on values that are claimed to be universal human values . . . claiming to demand only equal rights and equal consideration with no discrimination on the basis of sex. (pp. 354–357)

Liberal feminists search for equality in the existing system, desiring to participate and access both resources and gains without the need to change the modus operandi of the system. Traditional Marxists

believe that women are oppressed in their exclusion from public production . . . see knowledge as emerging through practical human involvement in changing the world, an involvement which also changes human beings themselves . . . [view] knowledge as socially constructed . . . and growing out of a specific mode of production. (pp. 354–357).

Traditional Marxists understand that by having equal access to the means of production, the system and the worker or participant are likely to change. Radical feminism "sees women's oppression consisting primarily in the universal male control of women's sexual and procreative capacities . . . [and] believes women know much of which men are ignorant and it takes one of its main tasks as being to explain why this should be so" (p. 365). Radical feminists tend to essentialize gender and oppression, claiming superiority by nature of being female. Socialist feminists reframe Marxism, viewing "knowledge as a social and practical construct" where the "adequacy of any theory . . . should represent the world from the standpoint of women," where "it is possible to gain a less biased and more comprehensive view of reality than that provided either by established bourgeois science or by the male-dominated leftist alternatives to it" (pp. 369–371).

Socialist feminism highlights the interdependency between class and gender oppression, refusing to assume that once class disparities are addressed, all other inequities will quickly disappear. Jaggar privileges socialist feminism and believes there is a singular standpoint for theorizing and activism. Others may recognize the difficulty in maintaining just one standpoint as they apply these various ideologies to lived experience.

Chris Beasley (1999) categorizes different approaches to feminism by the ways in which each presents sexual difference. The first assumes sameness, "that men and women are much the same," where "women are admitted to 'humanity' as described by traditional thought and female oppression is characterized as the restriction of women's human potential" (p. 15). The second contends women are different from and complementary to men, challenging "the assumed hierarchy underlying this account of the sexes found in traditional Western social and political thought" and celebrating such difference (p. 16). The third "eschew[s] the sameness/difference dichotomy by shifting the focus of [its] analysis to the question of the organization and effects of power"; it "downplays the significance of the issue of the similarity or difference between men and women in favour of considering potential strategies which resist or destabilize sexual hierarchy" (pp. 16–17). The fourth prefers a framework of alliance or coalition: "Men and women are not so much the same in kind (in an ontological sense) as potential political allies and hence can be partners in allied (much the same) struggles" (p. 17). The last considers women to be superior: "This approach involves an inversion, rather than reworking, of the mainstream conception of the sexes as different but complementary"; this is "often (though not always) connected to a perception of women as innately, intrinsically pre-eminent" (p. 18). The similarities between Beasley and Jaggar are evident and these are consistent throughout the literature on feminism. The critical significance here is to comprehend the general sorting categories, critique their distinctions, and make these pliable instruments.

Chela Sandoval (1991) offers a topography that is not specifically for feminist theory yet is extremely useful in the development of oppositional consciousness, which she deems crucial in feminism. The first

element is "equal rights" consciousness, where a "subordinated group might argue that their differences—for which they have been assigned inferior status—are only in appearance, not reality" (pp. 12–13). To a certain degree an equal rights consciousness critiques what is deemed inferior and by what standards. The next consciousness is "revolutionary," where the "subordinated group claim their differences from those in power and call for a social transformation that will accommodate and legitimate those differences" (pp. 12–13). A revolutionary consciousness seeks to validate their differences as they change the social landscape. The third, "supremacism," allows those oppressed to claim their differences as the elements that prove their superiority. Supremacism leaves the direction of power intact and only inverts the hierarchy. As hooks (1984) adds, "Feminism is a struggle to end sexist oppression. Therefore, it is necessarily a struggle to eradicate the ideology of domination" (p. 24). The fourth consciousness, "separatism," provides rationalization for the separation from the mainstream to protect and cultivate that which makes the oppressed different. The fifth category for Sandoval is "differential consciousness," which she sees not as entirely separate from the rest but rather as working through or with the categories. She contends:

> Self-conscious agents of differential consciousness recognize one another as allies . . . differential consciousness permits the practitioner to choose tactical positions, that is, to self-consciously break and reform ties to ideology, activities which are imperative for the psychological and political practices that permit the achievement of coalition cross differences. (p. 15)

It is this last consciousness that offers most promise in debunking the assumed static nature of theory. If theory is truly to become the strategy for change, as Eaton (2003) implies, the knowers must have multiple tools at their disposal and be willing to reconceptualize the use of these tools beyond their intended purpose.

Joy James (2000) uses black feminism to append distinctions between liberal, radical, and socialist feminism, while alerting us to the fluidity of such categories:

> Liberal, radical, and revolutionary black feminisms are often reductively presented as ideologically unified and uniformly "progressive," while black feminisms are simultaneously viewed as having little impact beyond black women.
>
> Black feminisms that accept the political legitimacy of corporate state institutional and police power but posit the need for humanistic reform are considered liberal. Black feminisms that view (female and black) oppression as stemming from capitalism, neocolonialism, and the corporate state that enforces both are generally understood to be radical. Some black feminisms explicitly challenge state and corporate dominance and critique the privileged status of bourgeois elites among the "Left": those that do so by connecting political theory for radical transformation with political acts to abolish corporate state and elite dominance are revolutionary, where "'Revolutionary' denotes dynamic movement, rather than fixed stasis, within a political praxis relevant to changing material conditions and social consciousness." (p. 245)

James cautions her readers to be especially mindful of the "shape-shifting" nature of these standpoints and the ways in which conditions change how they are lived out. She also points out that black feminism is said to sit on the margins of mainstream culture; as a result, its position by default is assumed to be radical. Ideology cuts across race as well as gender; situating black feminism or Asian feminism or Muslim feminism as outside of ideology reifies essentialist categories of identity and decreases possibilities for coalition building.

The above typologies, topographies, and categorizations offer structures from which to build fusions of ideology and politics for a deeply critical and informed activism. Fend off tendencies to completely buy into any one theory; demand more from what knowledge can afford and what the intersection of these theories might provide. Be critical, ask the unasked, and do not underestimate your own

Positionality

how one is situated through the intersection of power and the politics of gender, race, class, sexuality, ethnicity, culture, language, and other social factors

Decentering

dislocation, displacement, and shifting away from certainty

interpretation as you develop pragmatic theoretical tools. Push for new insights that legitimate your **positionality** while simultaneously **decentering** what is considered truth to invite both unlearning and learning anew.

Feminism is about locating yourself, about creating your agency through theorizing, not about any one act, thought, struggle, or lens of gender, race, ethnicity, class, or sexual expression. Identity politics and power are much more complex and organic than the forms we commonly employ, so I propose we resist the inclination to fit into neat social categories and the assumed inherent consciousness these afford. Instead, let us engage in the search for meaning not in certainty but in ambiguity, in the nuanced spaces of layers and juxtapositions within theoretical concepts and their manifestation in everyday realities. As Anzaldúa (1999) emphasizes:

> The new *mestiza* copes by developing a tolerance for contradictions, a tolerance for ambiguity . . . That focal point or fulcrum, that juncture where the *mestiza* stands, is where phenomena tend to collide. It is where the possibility of uniting all that is separate occurs. This assembly is not one where severed or separated pieces merely come together. Nor is it a balancing of opposing powers. In attempting to work out a synthesis, the self has added a third element which is greater than the sum of its severed parts. That third element is a new consciousness—a *mestiza* consciousness—and though it is a source of intense pain, its energy comes from continual creative motion that keeps down the unitary aspect of each new paradigm. (pp. 101–102)

Therefore, first embrace the idea of knowing in order to question and reconstruct what knowing in the service of our own emancipatory practices and our work toward social transformation may be. As one remains conscious or suspicious through "the project of making oneself intelligible, it is as useful to recognize forces to which one is *not* yielding as it is to recognize forces by which one is being shaped or immobilized" (Frye, 1993, p. 109). This mode of

theorizing challenges who is and works at being a cultural worker and public intellectual.

■ ■ ■

Feminist Theories and Education: A Primer maps history, foundations, theories, discourses, research analyses, and pedagogies through an insurgent need to debunk monolithic presentations of knowledge and discoveries. Special attention is paid to understanding the network of aligned discourses and disciplines that work in tandem against inequity and discrimination. The book provides accessible pathways to inhabiting feminism. Its salient feature is the adamant call to find comfort in the ambiguous, complex, messy, nuanced space of the **border dweller** (Anzaldúa's term), the space where individual agency is solidified through a political understanding of collective consciousness, power, and resistance, where there is recognition of temporality and transition in the search for meaning, belonging, and competence (similar to Rebecca Carver's ABC of experiential education discussed in Chapter Five). To champion uncertainty in a world where identities bank on absolute knowledge may seem contemptible; however, ambiguity more accurately represents the reality we inhabit as we move around, in, and out of multiple spaces daily.

The following chapters cover a variety of ideas I see as pertinent to a **reconceptualization** of feminist theories that more aptly captures the intricate relationships between gender, race/ethnicity, class, culture, sexual identity, religion/faith, language, positionality, power, and privilege. Such a reconceptualization does not attempt to disregard or rewrite existing research and literature; rather, its intent is to expand our interpretation and use of theory as different ideas come to bear on increasing our intellectual flexibility.

In Chapter Two, I chronicle the people and events that laid important foundations for theorizing and activism. I include what are generally con-

---

Border dweller

a person who straddles or lives across two or more borders (literal, theoretical, social, cultural, geographic, political, etc.)

Reconceptualization

restructuring based on reinterpretation of experience, history, and events as interdependent; a movement in curriculum studies reclaiming/ re-energizing subjectivity as central to learning and schooling

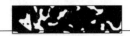

sidered central phenomena in the history of feminist thinking as well as other junctures that are equally important but often marginalized. I find it particularly important to highlight how both women and (some) men made their controversial and countercultural ideas public through speeches, writings, and actions, despite heavy costs, sacrifices, and disappointments. The chapter concludes by revisiting the purpose of theory and presents how feminist theory split into different factions.

Chapter Three covers contemporary discourses of gender studies, masculinity studies, queer studies, transnational studies, and visual studies, with special focus on the ways in which these problematize and stretch feminist theories. Through this cross-pollination of ideas and politics, our understanding of feminist theories is primed for new embodiments of consciousness and praxis. It is this **intertextuality** that creates new possibilities for research. I then switch to thought-provoking areas of study already within feminism, such as body studies (inclusive of sports and feminism, and sports sociology), ecofeminism, and virtual gender/cyberfeminism. The last two sections of the chapter discuss youth as docents of future feminist thinking and action and provide a brief overview of some national and international feminist collectives.

Chapter Four discusses feminist research analysis and the uses of theory to inform a variety of inquiry practices and dispositions. My concern here is with how feminist research analyses and methodologies can change actual social landscapes (public spaces, cultural norms, economic/educational access, and policy). I use the **trickster** as a research tool and figure for the border dweller. The trickster becomes a crucial agent of duplicity or ambiguity throughout the chapter to push our inquiries in critical and politically transformative ways. The chapter is structured through various elements of research, including epistemology/ideology, subjectivity/positionality, the politics of recognition, and action. These elements were fine-tuned in practice through a course co-taught with Dr. Kathy Jamieson,

Intertextuality
the ways a text references other texts and requires the engagement of the reader for multiple interpretations

Trickster
a mythic or folkloric figure who uses antagonism and uncertainty in breaking cultural codes

director of Women's and Gender Studies and associate professor in Exercise and Sport Science. Our collaboration in developing and teaching a graduate feminist research analysis course forced us to think through crucial factors in studying and maneuvering research, with the ultimate goal of using it for political and social change. From this work and process, students are better equipped to understand their position and direction in feminist research.

Chapter Five addresses feminist pedagogy, service learning, and experiential education to bridge alleged gaps between knowing and doing. Feminist pedagogy is critically analyzed for its promises and pitfalls, and it is problematized and reflected upon through my curricular experiences. I borrow the term **happenings** from the art world to illustrate the creative, dynamic, spontaneous pedagogical moments in constructed feminist learning communities. A critical post-structural feminist pedagogy then emerges to invoke Sandoval's differential consciousness and Anzaldúa's *mestiza* consciousness. I dedicate the last part of the chapter to discussing activism, its straightforward definition and possibilities to re-energize the desire in learning spaces and public places for a continued commitment to unequivocal engaged action.

Happenings

creative, multidisciplinary, carefully planned yet spontaneous and flexible events or performances in the art world

Last, but not least, I provide a compendium of resources for further inquiry and inspiration. I have grouped these thematically and by type for easy identification. These provide a wide array of springboards and invite you to continue the search for other sources of information.

One important point to remember is that despite the ambitious project of this primer to cover many topics and stretch feminist theories and education beyond their established borders, it remains porous and open. It stands as a marker of partial knowledge in a space–time continuum. I contribute to the conversation but do not present my contribution as a substitution of one master narrative for another. In fact, to do so would erode my insistent call to live in the nuance and accept the temporal nature of what we know when we know it. I invite you to

converse with me, to teach me as much as this book and my ideas may teach you. It is collaboration in critical inquiry and praxis around political issues that matter most to each of us and that I privilege most.

GLOSSARY

Agency—an individual's ability to self-advocate and critically negotiate complex power relations

Border dweller—a person who straddles or lives across two or more borders (literal, theoretical, social, cultural, geographic, political, etc.)

Decentering—dislocation, displacement, and shifting away from certainty

Differential consciousness—Chela Sandoval's term for consciousness (method) that allows movement between and among ideological and identity positions, requiring reading power manifestations and using whatever ideology is necessary for resistance

Happenings—creative, multidisciplinary, carefully planned yet spontaneous and flexible events or performances in the art world

Intertextuality—the ways a text references other texts and requires the engagement of the reader for multiple interpretations

Mestiza consciousness—Gloria Anzaldúa's term for the embodiment of developing a tolerance for contradictions and ambiguity produced by complex identity politics and heritage, living at the crossroads of multiple realities

Positionality—how one is situated through the intersection of power and the politics of gender, race, class, sexuality, ethnicity, culture, language, and other social factors

Praxis—a spiral in which critical reflection and action continuously inform each other in the service of individual and personal transformation, central to liberatory education

Reconceptualization—restructuring based on reinterpretation of experience, history, and events as interdependent in a continuum of time and space; a movement in curriculum studies reclaiming/re-energizing subjectivity as central to learning, the creation of curriculum, and the recognition of the social and political realities of schooling

Rhizome—a root; used here as a metaphor for a network of connections between concepts and entities

Trickster—a mythic or folkloric figure who uses antagonism and uncertainty in breaking cultural codes

Foundations of Feminist Theories

Mapping Ideas, People, and Events

Feminism is informed by the intersections of history, theory, ideology, social movements, and individual acts of courage and agency. Its foundations are in diverse struggles over labor, livelihood, health care, suffrage, access, and recognition. Women have fought to matter in the social contexts they inhabit—some through and within traditional roles, and others despite them. In mapping the origins of feminist theories in this chapter, we travel the varied paths of feminist work and delve into the struggles of women and men who wanted to make a social and political difference through the restructuring of gender rights.

The timeline that follows covers the early 1600s (with a brief visit to the first decade of the 1500s) to the early 2000s, spanning almost five centuries of feminist thinking and activism. Many of the figures, events, writings, speeches, and meetings discussed here centered on championing one social register or another, be it gender, race, class, or sexu-

ality. Fewer moments in history bring together two or more of these markers of identity and positionality. The recounting of history is fraught with human flaws, blinders, and conditional advocacy (which I explain in Chapter Five), so as you engage with historical figures, events, and ideas remain suspicious and inquisitive of what is unsaid, undocumented, and simplified. What follows is an ambitious seedbed for provocations. The chapter concludes with queries about the purpose of theory and a short exposition of plural perspectives in feminist theory.

1600s–1700s

The 1600s and 1700s colonial United States provided settlers with many challenges and opportunities for exploring individual capacity, gender roles, and expectations, while envisioning new ways of being. Unfortunately, this uncertainty was negotiated mostly through fear and abuse of power. The establishment and colonization of "new" territory gave way to oppressive practices; Native Americans and Mexicans already on North American soil were removed, displaced, endangered, and almost decimated, and many immigrants came to the United States as indentured servants, slaves, or brides-to-be. Some "free" women displayed great ingenuity during this period, taking advantage of numerous jobs and entrepreneurial opportunities inside and outside the home, such as providing apothecary and midwifery services, general health care, and food preparation. Many others did not adapt well to the survival needs of the "new world." The earliest record of English occupation dates from the late 1500s, when Roanoke Colony was established off the coast of North Carolina. Here Eleanor White Dare, John White's daughter, gave birth to the first English child, Virginia Dare, to be born on new world soil. In 1607, John Smith and a group of English settlers encountered the Powhatan Confederacy, a conglomeration of tribes in the eastern part of Virginia. In 1613, English colonists kid-

napped Pocahontas of the Mattaponi tribe for more than a year; during this time, she was baptized and married John Rolfe. Subsequently, and shortly before her death, Pocahontas became something of an ambassador between Virginia and England.

A century earlier, and on the opposite coast of North America, another important figure's history unfolded. La Malinche, born into a ruling Aztec family, was sold to another tribe after her father's death and later given to Hernan Cortes in 1519. La Malinche was multilingual and was Cortes's interpreter, negotiator, slave, and mistress. How active an agent she was in these negotiations has been the catalyst for rich historical research and literary work. Some regard her as a traitor; others as a negotiator between many indigenous groups and the Spanish conquerors. I briefly mention La Malinche as a parallel to Pocahontas—both iconic figures—to help us question neatly organized historical timelines and the pivotal role women have had in the production and reproduction of power. Despite the appearance of submissive positions in history, women have continued to strategically negotiate these limited spaces and thus it is these nuances that need closer study.

Nanye-hi (Nancy Ward) fought alongside her first husband in the Battle of Taliwa in 1755. He was killed, and she continued fighting until victory was won. This led to her appointment as one of the last Beloved Women of the Cherokee Nation before the twentieth century. As such, she sat on the General Council, headed the Women's Council, and negotiated treaties. Cherokee life slowly changed from communal to individual farming, with an increased need for labor. Nanye-hi is said to have been the first Cherokee to own black slaves; despite this, she is considered an early representative of feminist politics.

Jumping to the start of the Revolutionary War in the mid-1770s, we encounter another historic figure, Abigail Adams, who petitioned her husband, John Adams, to be conscious of gender differences as he drafted the Declaration of Independence. Her letter titled "Remember the Ladies" warned her hus-

band that if women were not considered, they would rebel against the laws that had not extended them any representation. She was clear that many men were inherently domineering and apt to abuse their power. Abigail used great foresight, requesting protection for women and collaboration with women in writing from her husband. She preferred women and men to work in partnership as the country progressed. John Adams, amused by Abigail's determination, attempted to lessen her concern by stating that men's power was largely an illusion since the reality was that women made decisions in the home. But Abigail was discussing power in public life, not domestic power relations.

Mercy Otis Warren shared many of the same concerns and was considered one of the most important intellectuals of the Revolution. She adopted a masculine pen name ("A Columbian Patriot") to publish many political editorials proposing ideas on governmental organization and leadership. Warren questioned whether politics was really her place as a woman, and it was John Adams who encouraged her to continue, believing she had a particular talent for political analysis. What disturbed Warren most was her need to adopt a male pen name to have access to a public forum. During the Revolutionary War, some women fought alongside their husbands and others enlisted in the army using male names. Some were discovered and discharged; others remained and fought alongside other soldiers, even receiving pensions for their military service (Hymowitz & Weissman, 1978). Throughout the decade John and Abigail were apart, she wrote many letters stressing the need for gender equality, especially in access to education and political rights. After her husband's dismissive response to her specific claims in "Remember the Ladies," she found great friendship and intellectual camaraderie with Mercy Otis Warren.

In 1790, Judith Sargent Murray wrote "On the Equality of the Sexes," in which she championed the intellectual capacity of women and presented a poignant commentary on the inequity in the social-

ization process between men and women. She contended that the focus on men's strength is a compensation for women's superior intellect. Murray was a strong believer in Universalism, a religion attempting to unite people across different faith systems to reach salvation.

In 1792, Mary Wollstonecraft's *A Vindication of the Rights of Woman* was published. In the book, which was considered an important feminist treatise, she addressed the assumed intellectual inferiority of women and overall incapacity to function or contribute socially, economically, or culturally. Wollstonecraft criticized the way women were treated as adornment, objects of desire, physically weak, and powerless. She hoped her words would position women in a progressive state with potential and possibility, not limitation. Wollstonecraft was a proponent of education for women, seeing it as a vehicle of social change. If indeed women were to have a social role (and in the case of Wollstonecraft I am not entirely sure that she always meant outside of traditional roles), they needed to have access to information so they could make their own informed decisions. She brought great attention to existing double standards, including legal ones, in late eighteenth-century society. Wollstonecraft, of the same mind as Abigail Adams, believed that men were inherently tyrannical, and that if men understood the discriminatory nature of the laws they authored, this would prove that their agenda departed from their rhetoric of independence and justice for all.

1800s

In the first half of the 1800s women's collegiate education was established, with the opening of the Troy Female Seminary in New York, Oberlin College in Ohio, Mount Holyoke College in Massachusetts, and the Female Medical College of Philadelphia. A recurrent complaint in the important documents I include in this narrative history is the unequal access to education for girls, young women, and women. Education is consistently regarded as a vehicle for

social change and mobility and the development of formidable intellect.

Much like La Malinche and Pocahontas, Sacagawea found herself as interloper, guide, and negotiator between cultures. Originally from the Shoshone, at ten or eleven she was taken by the Minitaree and sold to Toussaint Charbonneau. Lewis and Clark hired Charbonneau to accompany them on their expedition, and Sacagawea went as well. Her role and relationship with regard to Clark have been the source of much historical, feminist, and literary research, once again marking the interest in individuals who are caught or torn between multiple cultures and power dynamics.

During the 1830s, the Grimké sisters (Angelina and Sarah) wrote prolifically on both abolition and women's rights. They were committed abolitionists and activists, traveling the country to denounce slavery and racial prejudice. Part of their argument was targeted particularly at white women, openly discussing how slavery destroyed the institution of marriage and condemning the rape of slaves. They met great resistance and personal attacks, quickly turning these into more fuel for activism. They exposed the socially constructed process by which women are portrayed as decoration, dependent on and inferior to men. In contrast, men were portrayed as strong warriors, stern, proud, and in control. The sisters were very critical of religious texts and their interpretations, particularly when women were regarded as gifts to men. They argued that this reinforced the notion that women were a possession and subject to the will of men, making equal rights all the more necessary. Among their works are *Appeal to the Christian Women of the South* in 1836 by Angelina, *Epistle to the Clergy of the Southern States* in 1836 by Sarah, *Appeal to the Women of the Nominally Free States* in 1837 by Angelina, *Letters to Catharine Beecher* in 1837 by Angelina (Beecher was appalled the young women were speaking out publicly), *Letters on the Equality of the Sexes* in 1837 by Sarah, and *American Slavery as It Is: Testimony of a Thousand Witnesses* in 1839, edited by both sisters.

Some say Sarah leaned more toward feminist arguments and Angelina toward abolitionist ones. They truly spoke and wrote on both, often interlacing the numerous issues of race and gender. Regardless, both were prolific and commanding writers who were mobilized by social conditions and humanitarian convictions. The sisters were often warned not to conflate feminism and abolitionism or to champion them together, in fear that the fight for women's rights would halt anti-slavery action. To the Grimké sisters, both groups, women and slaves, had been denied the rights granted to all by the Constitution; therefore they saw it as a duty to act on both issues.

Margaret Fuller, a writer and journalist, published *The Great Lawsuit: Man versus Men; Woman versus Women* in 1843 and *Woman in the Nineteenth Century* in 1845, which is regarded as a feminist classic. One of her main points was that men and women should have the same rights, not because either sex already received special privileges but because she regarded men and women as partners and collaborators in a greater social context. She highlighted the conditional aspects of the rhetoric of freedom in the new world and contended freedom should be realized by all its members, not reserved only for free men.

From the 1820s through the 1840s, mostly young women from their teens to their thirties from rural parts of the country gained other opportunities to work outside the home with the development of looms and textile mills, paving the way for the popularity of the factories. Women working at the mills were often regarded as either mill girls or female operatives. Acceptable employment for women until this point in history had been mainly in education or domestic work that paid even less than working at the textile mills. Many women saw this new type of work as an avenue to independence. They would live in boardinghouses (with strict curfews and guidelines for moral conduct) and work at the mills until they saved enough money to sustain themselves. Women were considered perfectly suited

for mill jobs and were more economical for mill owners, sometimes earning half of men's salaries for longer shifts.

Many young women used their few free hours to learn, capitalizing on free lectures offered in the city and seeking any other opportunities for self-improvement. The young women formed "improvement circles" (many associated with churches), where they would exchange and critique their writing for future publication. The long hours, low pay, increased productivity expectations, and substandard working conditions led some to develop poignant critiques of labor. By 1845 several publications had surfaced (*Factory Tracts, Factory Girl, Factory Girls' Album, Lowell Offering,* and *Voice of Industry*) exposing the disparities and inequities within the system of textile mills in Lowell, Massachusetts, and other parts of New England. Women were asked to examine and compare their working conditions, stressing the normative intents of substandard labor structures and practices. The late 1830s saw national economic strife as a result of the depression. The following excerpts are taken from *Factory Tracts*:

> Shall the worthy laborer be awed into silence by wealth and power, and for fear of being deprived of the means of procuring his daily bread? Shall tyranny and cruel oppression be allowed to rived the chains of physical and mental slavery . . . Slaves to a system of labor . . . slaves to the will and requirements of the "powers that be," . . . slaves to ignorance—and how can it be otherwise? What time has the operative to bestow on moral, religious or intellectual culture? . . . Common sense will each every one the utter impossibility of improving the mind under these circumstances, however great the desire may be for knowledge. (An Operative, 1845a).
>
> Reader will you pronounce this a mere fancy sketch, written for the sake of effect? It is not so. It is a real picture of "Factory life" . . . why, if these evils are so aggravating, have they been so long and so peacefully borne? . . . we would call upon every operative in *our* city . . . to awake from the lethargy which has fallen upon them, and assert and maintain their rights. We will call upon you for action—*united and immediate action* . . . [with]

the Female Labor Reform Association . . . we will soon show these *drivelling* cotton lords, this mushroom aristocracy of New England, who so arrogantly aspire to lord it over God's heritage, that our rights cannot be trampled upon with impunity; that we WILL not longer submit to that arbitrary power. . . . (An Operative, 1845b)

This outrage worked as a mobilizing agent to get more people involved and make them aware of poor employment conditions. Harriet Farley proposed education as a method through which to compensate for the system of the textile mills, more as an escape from it than as to gain tools for combating inequity. She was not advocating a critique of power or hierarchy in the mills; on the contrary, she saw the working conditions as something out of the workers' control. Her writing came out of her participation in the improvement circles. Farley became a regular contributor to the *Lowell Offering,* leaving the textile mill to co-edit the literary magazine full time. She also joined the anti-slavery society and was an adamant advocate for the abolition of slavery. Her friend and labor reform activist Sarah Bagley criticized her apolitical writing and editing of the *Lowell Offering,* which was publicly criticized for representing corporate values and ideas. Other papers and magazines lent a clearer critical perspective on labor reform. Bagley was a strong supporter of reducing the workday to ten hours for women and men laborers, as well as improving working conditions overall. She founded the Lowell Female Reform Association. Farley, influenced by Bagley, closed the magazine. A few years later she started the *New England Offering,* which she edited and published, and where a more active reformist voice was established, not just on labor issues but on slavery and other pressing social issues of the time.

Bagley became editor of *The Voice of Industry* in 1846, where she continued her reform efforts. After being too successful in her organizing efforts, she was fired from the paper. Shortly thereafter, she worked for the telegraph company, a new technol-

ogy, and secured an equitable place for women and men to work. Bagley soon discovered she earned one third of what men earned; disconcerted, she returned to Lowell for new opportunities. During the 1850s and 1860s, she and her husband specialized in homeopathic medicine, charging the rich a small fee and rendering free services to the poor. She continued her writing on labor reform but also wrote on health care and education. The ten-hour workday she so fervently fought for was not enforced until the 1870s—and even then, rather sporadically, as many mill owners found ways around such mandates. Unfortunately, many feminists of the time did not lend their support to the working women's reform efforts. This foreshadowed the ardent struggles between working-class and middle-class perspectives in feminism.

It was in 1848 in Seneca Falls, New York, when Elizabeth Cady Stanton convened a group of interested women and men (more than 300 people, young and old) to discuss the social, civic, and religious rights of women and potential strategies for change. She wanted to issue a Declaration of Rights and Sentiments in much the same vein as the Declaration of Independence from 1776. This group intended to rectify the omissions Abigail Adams had warned against decades earlier, specifically addressing the differences in the exercise of power by men over women. The Declaration of Sentiments identified twelve rights for women, including the right to vote, to wealth and to earn wages, to employment, to own property, to education, to hold public office, and to be equal to men in every way. Lucretia Mott (later noted as one of the "mothers" of the feminist movement) and Frederick Douglass were also part of the convention. Both Stanton and Mott attended the Anti-Slavery Convention in 1840, even though women were excluded from participating in the proceedings. In fact, it is said that their experiences at the Anti-Slavery Convention fueled the convention for women's rights. At the 1840 convention they were discriminated against because of their gender, despite the universal emancipation goal.

After the Seneca Falls convention, several groups held annual meetings across the nation. Lucy Stone marveled crowds with her vehement assertions of women's capacity to function in society being equal to men's and emphatically resisted the recurring inference that anything women did diminished the value of men's roles. She was the first woman to graduate with a college degree in Massachusetts, from Oberlin College.

In 1844, Paulina Wright Davis began lecturing on women's bodies, health, and sexual issues. At the time, she was one of the few public figures who would engage such issues and educate women about their own bodies. The public discourse of the time was highly restricted by practices of civility and politeness. In 1853 she started what some say was the first feminist newspaper, *The Una*. Others say it was Amelia Bloomer, who in 1849 founded and edited *The Lily,* the first newspaper to be concerned with women's equality. Bloomer is more widely known for advocating a new style of dress for women. In 1871 Davis wrote *A History of the National Women's Rights Movement,* and she was instrumental in making the medical field accessible to women, urging women to become physicians.

In 1851, Sojourner Truth gave her "Ain't I a Woman?" speech at a women's convention in Ohio. In this brief speech, she forecast a backlash when dominant society realized both blacks and women were mobilizing for their denied rights. Sojourner Truth also made an important observation of both class and racial discrimination in her discussion of men's insistence on women needing help, where she stressed it was white women who were assisted, not blacks or any other woman of color. She noted that her physical strength was equal to a man's and asked the audience whether that made her any less a woman. Slightly more than a decade later, the 13th Amendment to the U.S. Constitution ended slavery and made way for many women-led organizations focusing specifically on racial consciousness.

Shortly thereafter Elizabeth Cady Stanton, Susan B. Anthony, and Frederick Douglass organized the

American Equal Rights Association aimed at accomplishing universal suffrage. In 1869, Stanton and Anthony formed the National Woman Suffrage Association in New York in reaction to the 14th Amendment, which defines citizenship and voting as solely male rights, and the 15th Amendment, which grants black men the right to vote. Susan B. Anthony was notably upset over the change to the Constitution, and many of her writings in response positioned white women as superior to black and immigrant men. Her racist retaliations speak to the divisive tactics of power and the common inability to work in solidarity through many obstacles. Consequently, there was a split in the association, and Julia Ward Howe, Lucy Stone, and Henry Blackwell created the American Woman Suffrage Association in Boston, continuing the collaborative fight of anti-slavery and women's rights. The fight and struggle over women's right to vote grew stronger and unfortunately further divided many allies as a result of black men's access to voting. This split lasted more than twenty years. Some saw the right to vote as the key to equality; Stanton, in particular, had a better understanding of the oppressive system of power. She saw the right to vote as just one stepping-stone in a much larger fight for equality. In hopes of raising consciousness, women tried to vote whenever the opportunity arose and were usually arrested or turned away. After the Civil War, Stanton and Anthony joined forces with George Train, a man of questionable racial politics but a supporter of women's suffrage. Train provided the funds for Stanton and Anthony's feminist newspaper, *The Revolution,* a weekly paper with coverage of local and national issues written by and for women. The paper became a platform for feminist theorizing and practice, critically discussing economic independence and equity, physical strength, access to education, reformation of marriage and divorce, health education, and religious dogma. The source of funding did not seem to raise any ethical questions for the two women, nor did their lack of popularity with working women, despite their efforts to raise awareness on various women's plights across the nation. The paper eventually was closed as a result of Train's ostentatious activity. Stanton and Anthony tried to finance the paper themselves but were in the end unsuccessful. Despite the closing of the paper, they continued to write and speak on issues affecting women in the late 1800s. In 1890 the two women's suffrage organizations united again under the new title of the National American Woman Suffrage Association (NAWSA), led by Stanton. Around the same time, Stanton published *The Woman's Bible,* which provides an analysis of women's roles in organized religions and places of worship. She believed organized religion and traditional customs were major culprits in women's oppression. Shortly afterward, Stanton resigned from NAWSA following much criticism for her recent work.

While Stanton and Anthony struggled for suffrage in the east, women in Wyoming were granted the right to vote (Utah, Colorado, and Idaho would soon follow). Esther Hobart Morris (the first woman to be appointed justice of the peace), who is mostly credited for this political milestone, convinced legislators of the civil benefits of giving women the right to vote, allowing them to become full partners in the development of the west. Along with the right to vote, white women gained rights to own property and equal salaries in the teaching profession. The west, considerably less populated than the northeast or southeast, was next to conquer. Many women moved west, escaping the strict Victorian standards for femininity. Through the Homestead Act of 1862, the west, already a complex territory of removal and occupation, provided the means for many white women to gain independence. The act offered 160 acres of free land to both white women and men who would commit to at least five years of residency and farming in the west. There was no mention of what assistance was necessary or provided for women to succeed or of what would occur if they did not. Most other women—Native Americans, Mexicans, Mexican Americans, and Chinese—did not have

access to these benefits; they were taken advantage of physically and economically and used as property in violent exchanges between whites moving westward and existing residents.

The Civil War was in full force in the early 1860s. Many southern women were left to keep work and home life going; other southern women, disguised as men, joined the war; still others became couriers or spies and performed all sorts of jobs connected with warfare. Harriet Tubman freed herself with the help of a few white individuals and returned to the south time and time again to bring numerous slaves to freedom. Her perseverance and ingenuity made possible something unthinkable and unlawful, yet her activism was not claimed under the auspices of feminism (then), even though some feminists were active in the anti-slavery movement. In 1863, Stanton and Anthony turned their efforts to the Emancipation Proclamation, forming the National Women's Loyal League, the sole purpose of which was to petition Congress for a constitutional amendment prohibiting slavery. After the war ended, living conditions in the south became increasingly difficult, as women were expected to shift their obligations and duties through redefined gender roles (out of necessity) in their private spheres while retaining a lady's decorum in public. The consequences of the war increased racial strife and economic disparity and limited access to education and property ownership. The south was not going to change gender roles, racial discrimination, or class hierarchy willingly.

Frances Ellen Watkins Harper, a writer from Baltimore, was the first black woman to publish a novel. Her writing is particularly important, even though it is not theoretical in nature. Harper researched her subjects extensively, traveling through the south to study and write about black life. She found great strength in the family structure and a distinct push for knowledge, access to education, and development of intelligence. She describes women emphasizing this as a prerequisite to be able to capitalize on the few rights they had. Her

writings, despite being creative (mainly in the forms of novels and poetry), exhibit keen social analysis of black southern life as white supremacy gained momentum.

In 1862, Mary Jane Patterson became the first African American to graduate from Oberlin College with a bachelor's degree. She dedicated her life to the education of African American youth as an educator and principal of several schools in Washington, DC.

Many northern white women called for recognition of their contribution to the war efforts and proposed their right to vote as compensation, forging the various efforts to secure women's suffrage. In 1874, Annie Wittenmyer was elected the first president of the Woman's Christian Temperance Union (WCTU), whose main focus was on banning the consumption of alcoholic beverages to protect the home. Wittenmyer established *Our Union,* the WCTU's journal, and edited *Home and Country,* the organization's magazine. She also wrote *History of the Women's Temperance Crusade* in 1878 and *Women of the Reformation* in 1884. The WCTU took on the fight for women's suffrage when Francis Willard was elected president in the organization's sixth year. Willard's focus turned to doing anything possible to help women and children, making the WCTU a significant social reform agency. Willard, critiqued by other feminists for her strategies, advocated for women's traditional role in the home. This was perceived as a dangerous argument reifying the assumption of women's position in society. Catherine Beecher made similar arguments in pushing for women's professionalization in teaching, education, and social life. Beecher argued for these based on women's alleged innate capacity to be better nurturers and caretakers. Willard upheld a core belief of the WCTU to protect the home from a variety of social ills, mainly liquor consumption. Many women who might not otherwise have turned to feminism did so as a result of their support of restricting liquor consumption. Before joining the WCTU, Willard was president of Evanston College for Ladies in 1871,

and in 1873 became the first dean of women at Northwestern University and professor of esthetics. During this time she was also a journalist and an editor of the *Chicago Daily Post*. After Willard's death, the WCTU lessened its involvement with suffrage, deeming it unimportant in comparison to prohibition.

In 1878, the 19th Amendment was introduced in Congress advocating for women's right to vote, yet it was not ratified until 1920. Jane Addams and Ellen Gates Starr opened Hull House in 1889 and refocused social concerns on women, children, and families. Addams wrote prolifically about Hull House's programs, initiatives for the settlement house movement, and civil rights. Much of her writing on youth was problematic though, conflating issues of class and adolescence. She supported the assumptions of Social Darwinists (particularly G. Stanley Hall) that immigrant and poor youth were inherently deviant and in need of social control. In 1931 she was awarded the Nobel Peace Prize. In a speech about suffrage, she contended, "I am not one of those who believe—broadly speaking—that women are better than men. We have not wrecked railroads, nor corrupted legislatures, nor done many unholy things that men have done; but then we must remember that we have not had the chance."[1] During the early 1890s many other activists, reformers, and scholars came to Hull House to work and receive some assistance themselves. One of them was Florence Kelley, a young upper-middle-class woman educated at the University of Zurich for graduate studies and a former college friend of Addams. She was a member of the Socialist Party and was appointed to the State Bureau of Labor Statistics to study factories in Chicago. It was Kelley who encouraged Addams to take on a greater social purpose through Hull House and to work to end poverty. Kelley's objective was social reform, not temporary solutions.

Victoria Claflin Woodhull and Frederick Douglass were nominated as president and vice president for the Equal Rights Party in 1872. Some saw this as a way to reunite abolitionists and suffragists and refocus their collaborative civil rights work. Woodhull was a controversial figure for her writing and advocacy on political and social reform, especially for her support of free love, sex education, and eugenics; she and her sister, Tennessee, were the first women to become stockbrokers on Wall Street. Victoria Woodhull was the first to publish Marx and Engels's *The Communist Manifesto.* Victoria and Tennessee established their own newspaper, *Woodhull and Claflin's Weekly,* in 1870. Both sisters questioned the power hierarchy established in marriage practices and restricted sexual behaviors within traditional relationships. Woodhull believed women should have the same sexual freedom men did. The sisters were strong advocates for women to gain knowledge about their bodies, health, and choice. Victoria was often persecuted for her ideas on free love, though she did not advocate sexual promiscuity. She scandalized repressive Victorian decorum and soon was marginalized in New York society. Some suffragists feared "free love" would delay progress on the right to vote. The sisters were jailed for "circulating an obscene publication," an issue of the *Woodhull and Caflin's Weekly* in which the sisters denounced an affair between Henry Ward Beecher (Catharine Beecher's husband) and Elizabeth Tilton (wife of a preacher) in retaliation for their persecution. They were eventually released and the charges were dropped, but the sisters were deeply affected and dramatically changed. Both sisters retreated, married, and converted to a religious life, a definite turn from their activism on sexual freedom and sexual education. The sacrifices and consequences of speaking against the norm, of having economic freedom, and of having access to the world of public ideas are sometimes unbearable when it is clear that the personal becomes political. During the late 1800s, society was even less prepared to deal with self-sufficient women unrestrained by middle-class values who wanted to change lived experiences for single and married women of all ages.

From the 1880s to the late 1920s, Mary Harris Jones, a.k.a. Mother Jones, was a labor activist and reformer. She worked as a teacher and seamstress before and after the death of her four children and husband in a yellow fever epidemic that ravaged Memphis, Tennessee. She moved back to Chicago and opened a seamstress shop that burned in the Great Fire of 1871. Her displacement led her to an increased awareness of the labor movement and the Knights of Labor, a major union organization. In the 1920s, toward the end of her life, she wrote her autobiography; speaking about a strike in Virginia, she stated, "I do know that there are no limits to which powers of privilege will not go to keep the workers in slavery" (http://www.angelfire.com/nj3/RonMBaseman/mojones1.htm. In 1901 she wrote an article for the *International Socialist Review* titled "Civilization in Southern Mills" in which she denounces child labor. In her autobiography authored around 1922 or 1923 she wrote a chapter on child labor where, she states:

> I have always advised men to read. All my life I have told them to study the works of those great authors who have been interested in making this world a happier place for those who do its drudgery. When there were no strikes, I held educational meetings and after the meetings I would sell the book, "Merrie England," which told in simple fashion of the workers' struggle for a more abundant life. "Boys," I would say, "listen to me. Instead of going to the pool and gambling rooms, go up to the mountain and read this book. Sit under the trees, listen to the birds and take a lesson from those little feathered creatures who do not exploit one another, nor betray one another, nor put their own little ones to work digging worms before their time. You will hear them sing while they work." (http://www.angelfire.com/nj3/RonMBaseman/mojones2.htm)

She traveled the United States, going wherever she was called to help workers, miners, and child laborers organize and fight for more equitable working conditions. In 1898 she assisted in founding the Social Democratic Party and the Industrial Workers

of the World, and she was a part of the United Mine Workers Association. More important to those she fought for/with, she joined strike after strike with them and was arrested many times. Everywhere Mother Jones went she provided an education on labor history, rights, and negotiations.

In 1883, Sara Winnemucca was considered a pioneer for writing about the suffering and inequity suffered at the hands of the white man in "Life among the Piutes: Their Wrongs and Claims." She was a Piute Indian from Nevada who was repeatedly forced from her home and land with her family. She used her story as an appeal for understanding and as a way to bring awareness of the deplorable social conditions produced by abuses of power. She was also a public speaker, activist, and organizer, sharing her story and commentary across the United States and Europe. Sara also opened a school for Indian children called the Peabody's Institute. The school closed after the death of her husband, yet she continued to work as a cultural bridge between communities, tribes, and white settlers.

In 1896, Ida B. Wells, Mary Church Terrell, Margaret Murray Washington, Charlotte Forten Grimke, Fanny Jackson Coppin, Harriet Tubman, and Frances Ellen Watkins Harper formed the National Association of Colored Women's Clubs. Wells also helped to form the Niagara Movement, the predecessor to the National Association for the Advancement of Colored People. Always extremely vocal in the struggle against racial and gender discrimination and an activist against lynching, Wells wrote many editorials on the subject in the newspaper she co-owned, *The Free Speech and Headlight.* As a result, her life was threatened several times and the newspaper office was burned down. Wells moved to Illinois, where she continued writing and teaching, becoming a central figure in Chicago's gender and racial struggles. She authored *Southern Horrors: Lynch Law in All Its Phases, The Red Record,* and numerous articles. She criticized the exclusion of African Americans from the World's Columbian Exposition at Chicago's World Fair and the proposi-

tion for a separate fair for blacks. She continued her activism and organizing through her writing in the *Conservator* and the development of the Negro Fellowship League and Alpha Suffrage Club (with Belle Squire), the first black women's suffrage organization. In 1930 she ran for Illinois state senate hoping to make a greater difference in the fight against poverty and crime.

As a whole the American public remained resistant to feminist ideals. The implications of such public work were private changes to the way families operated and related, changes many were neither ready to make nor wanted to make. Lucy Stone urged "moral reform in marriage," where women's bodies would not be used as reproductive machines, and her solution was abstinence. She reconsidered her platform after marrying Henry Blackwell, a feminist and abolitionist. They joined forces to fight against discrimination, and their daughter continued their work, advocating more equal rights for property, access, and mainly over one's body (Hymowitz & Weissman, 1978).

The critique that feminism was about "bored or disappointed housewives or women in general" was used strategically by many feminist public speakers. Lucy Stone called for people to dwell on these feelings long enough to motivate change and equal rights for all women. Susan B. Anthony believed economic inequity was detrimental to the progress of women's rights. She stated:

> Women must have a purse of their own and how can this be so long as the wife is denied the right to her individual and joint earnings. Reflections like these caused me to see and really feel that there was no true freedom for woman without the possession of all her property rights, and that these rights could be obtained through legislation only. (cited in Hymowitz & Weissman, 1978, p. 116)

Regardless of marital status, women needed access to their own money for independence. Anthony worked diligently with Stanton to petition for the passage of the Married Woman's Property Act of 1848. This protected only women's property, not their earned wages. Anthony found this insufficient and worked tirelessly to win full property and wage rights. She would not be successful (for residents of New York) until 1860.

The General Federation of Women's Clubs started in Chicago around 1890. Its membership grew quickly to more than 1 million by 1910. Even though it was closely involved in the suffrage movement, it did not support racial unity. The organization adopted an anti-black policy in the early 1900s to secure white southern women's membership. When suffrage was imminent, the organization lost interest in many equity issues and turned its focus to leisure pastimes and self-improvement.

Charlotte Perkins Gilman began her writing career with her short story "The Yellow Wallpaper," which she wrote in 1892 while experiencing post-partum depression. Gilman is best known for *Women and Economics,* published in 1898, in which she addresses the antiquated division of social roles between men and women. She presented a clear case for understanding gender as a social construct not a biological one. Gilman believed, as did many others, that it was economic stability that would facilitate women's independence. She wrote many novels as well, gaining fame through her lecturing and writing on ethics, labor, and social equality. In 1909 she founded and edited her own journal, *The Forerunner.*

1900s

By the start of the twentieth century many labor organizations had developed; among these were the Women's Trade Union League and the International Ladies' Garment Workers' Union. The early 1900s saw an increase in the number of women workers, many of them immigrants. Many young women found jobs either as domestic workers or as factory workers in deplorable conditions. As in the previous century, many grew discontented and searched for ways to organize against working conditions through unions and the Socialist Party. For working women, the fight was not only about gender but about the

incredible abuse of power over the working class. Elizabeth Gurley Flynn, like Mother Jones, was part of numerous strikes around the nation, fulfilling her wish for a public/social life while helping in organizing reform and militant action. At the age of sixteen, Flynn made her first speech, "What Socialism Will Do for Women," for the Harlem Socialist Club. She continued public speaking and writing, starting a feminist column for the *Daily Worker* in 1936. She also wrote *The Rebel Girl* and *The Alderson Story: My Life As a Political Prisoner,* both in 1955. She was a founding member of the American Civil Liberties Union and a member of the Industrial Workers of the World.

Other women rose as leaders in the labor movement; among them was Bessie Abramowitz, who with her husband established the Amalgamated Clothing Workers of America to fight for forty-hour workweeks, child care, unemployment insurance, continuing education, health care, housing, and union banks. Abramowitz's work began with the Chicago garment workers' strike in 1910. Numerous strikes followed, the most notable being the Bread and Roses Strike of 1912 in Lawrence, Massachusetts. The strike, including more than 25,000 women, child, and men workers, lasted for ten weeks. Despite a very small reduction in work hours per week, factory owners made employees work faster for lower pay to compensate for the shortened workweek. The factory workers, the majority of whom were women, took to the streets, shouting "Short pay, short pay!" and "We want bread and roses too!" (Kornbluh, n.d.). This strike united immigrants from many countries. Strike leaders from the Industrial Workers of the World and the Italian Language Federation of the American Socialist Party were conscious that they should have appropriate representation from each country. Elizabeth Gurley Flynn came to be involved in the strike and was asked to help organize the workers. Strike leaders were successful in structuring the strategies for protest, and the Lawrence militia came out in full force with extreme acts of brutality. It was not until these acts were targeted

against children that a national outcry for an investigation occurred. Congress heard testimony after testimony on the substandard working conditions for all the workers. The factory owners finally conceded to all of the strikers' demands in fear of higher tariffs from the government. Those imprisoned waited much longer for justice, arguing against fabricated accounts of what had occurred during the strike, and were acquitted almost six months later. The strike demonstrated what was possible when workers united and organized.

The labor movement suffered greatly from gender discrimination, despite the substantial involvement and leadership of women in labor organizations and protests. Many women were disheartened by men's work negotiations, by the lack of understanding for equal pay and work, by differences in how women and men related publicly and privately, and by how socialist ideology fell short in transforming traditional gender roles and expectations. Emma Goldman (1911), often called upon to speak for the Socialist Party in the labor movement, explained in one of her essays, "Woman Suffrage," why gender and class inequities prevailed regardless of any law or policy. She discussed the complexity of power, seeing it as a system that manifests itself differently depending on the social, cultural, and political location of the individual or group and the narrow understanding that one act or legislation will change a culture, a systemic tradition. Regardless of the number of people that any current system disadvantages, there is great investment in keeping it as is among those it benefits. Goldman wrote extensively throughout her life in journals, books, and pamphlets; among her works are *Mother Earth* (journal), *Living My Life* (book), "Anarchy and the Sex Question," "The Place of Individual in Society," and "Socialism: Caught in the Political Trap" (articles).

Alice Paul and Lucy Burns established the National Woman's Party, whose activists publicly made their case for equal rights and women's suffrage. Along with Carrie Chapman Catt and NAWSA, an all-out campaign was undertaken to solidify

women's right to vote. Suffragettes worked furiously to secure the vote for women in 1920 and succeeded in the summer of that year. The National Woman's Party moved next on their agenda to the Equal Rights Amendment. NAWSA turned into the League of Women Voters.

Margaret Sanger opened the first birth control clinic in Brooklyn, New York, in 1913, after a trip to Europe, where she learned about the diaphragm and other research on contraception. New York authorities closed the clinic and subsequently arrested Sanger and her sister, Ethel Byrne. After Byrne's hunger strike, and when both had served a thirty-day sentence, they lobbied to delink birth control from obscenity laws. They succeeded and were able to open another clinic in New York, the Clinical Research Bureau, which dispensed birth control primarily to women whose health would be in jeopardy if they became pregnant again. In 1923, Sanger founded the American Birth Control League, which in 1942 was renamed Planned Parenthood.

Sanger is credited with organizing public awareness of birth control as a health issue and bringing safer contraception to women. Women at the time had limited methods for preventing unwanted pregnancies and equally limited education on sex and health issues. Sanger, a nurse, found herself helping many women recover from unsafe abortions or too many sequential births. She saw the need for safe and accessible birth control for women to have control over their own bodies and futures. The biggest hurdle for many women remained misinformation, or a lack of information, on a variety of health issues. Insufficient public education efforts were made to address the various communities' restricted access to accurate health information. Restrictions on dispensing birth control made it inaccessible and inconvenient for the majority of women in the 1920s and 1930s. It would take another several decades before a greater variety of contraception was accessible to the public.

The Equal Rights Amendment, written in 1921 by Alice Paul, demanded equal rights under the law on the basis of gender. This amendment has yet to be ratified, gaining the support of only thirty of the thirty-eight states required for ratification. It has been reintroduced to Congress every year after its expiration without success. That the push for equal rights followed soon after the granting of the right to vote further alienated African Americans and working women. For some, the right to vote was rendered unimportant given the plight of slavery, the abuse of women under such a system, and the labor reform strikes. Slaves were fighting to claim their will, their right over their own bodies, and the right to be considered fully human. They resisted in numerous ways, despite having little opportunity to organize against the systems of oppression. Women workers fought against child labor and demanded better working conditions.

But for a few important exceptions, feminism (at least as defined by popular consensus) arose from largely white middle-class concerns and struggles. During World War II more women went to work for manufacturers, the government, and the armed forces. The Equal Pay Act was presented in Congress in 1943 but did not pass until 1963; to this day women earn 77 cents for every dollar earned by men. The UN Commission on the Status of Women was established in 1946 to protect equal political rights, economic rights, and educational opportunities for women around the world.

The birth control movement changed public discourse about women's health and sexual lives. By the mid-1940s, women's sexuality was studied more intensely. Helen Deutsch authored *The Psychology of Women* and Marynia Farnham and Ferdinand Lundberg published *Modern Woman: The Lost Sex* in 1947. Psychoanalytic theory influenced these works tremendously, framing women's sex drives as only for reproductive and nurturing purposes. Any deviation from this superimposed limitation was subsequently pathologized. Many women argued for control over their own sexual and reproductive lives and thought equality could not be realized until this was attained.

Simone de Beauvoir wrote *The Second Sex* in 1949 (English translation 1953), in which she discussed feminism and women's subordinate role. She introduced gender as social construct and the **otherization** of women in society, refuting the marginalization of women. The book stressed that gender differences were the result of culture, not nature. de Beauvoir discovered, in her studies of self and society through philosophy, sociology, and psychology, how to deepen our understanding and analysis of power, particularly its impact on our selves and experiences.

Otherization
the process of marginalizing difference, most times through negative stigmas and stereotypes

In 1955 Rosa Parks, former secretary of the National Association for the Advancement of Colored People, refused to give up her seat on a bus to a white person (having become tired of the continuous discrimination of the time); she was arrested and put on trial. Before her arrest, two other young women, Claudette Colvin and Mary Louise Smith, fifteen and eighteen years old respectively, refused to give up their seats and were arrested. These events led to a long-overdue organized resistance. The Montgomery bus boycott ensued, marking a collective movement to protest segregation laws not only in the transportation system but community-wide. Sit-ins, freedom rides, and marches followed all across the nation.

Also in 1955, Del Martin and Phyllis Lyon cofound the Daughters of Bilitis (DOB), the first group in the United States to champion lesbian rights. For the most part, the contemporary feminist movement reinforced **heteronormativity;** consequently, there was a genuine need to debunk what and how norms were defined in the twentieth century.

Heteronormativity
the construction of heterosexuality as the pervasive norm in society, establishing a naturalization of sex and gender roles

In 1962 Dolores Huerta, along with César Chávez, co-found the United Farm Workers. She organized boycotts of the grape industry and lobbied for the Agricultural Labor Relations Act. Fannie Lou Hammer tried to get neighbors registered to vote and was arrested and beaten. She later helped create the Mississippi Freedom Democratic Party and mobilized for greater voter participation.

In 1964 Congress passed the Civil Rights Act and in 1965 the Equal Voting Rights Act.

Betty Friedan published *The Feminine Mystique* in 1963. This book is said to have instigated the second wave in feminism and the contemporary women's movement. Seldom is one incident the catalyst for an entire movement; more realistically, it is a sequence of events and a consensus of consciousness. A few years before the publication of Friedan's book, Esther Peterson, who headed the Women's Bureau of the Department of Labor, asked President Kennedy to address gender discrimination. He then asked Eleanor Roosevelt to chair a Commission on the Status of Women. This group researched and documented rampant discrimination against women throughout society. Such work at the federal level motivated local governments to look into the situation in their own states. In *The Feminine Mystique,* Friedan focused on one sphere of gender differences, the family, and critiqued the construction of domesticity in middle-class America, specifically the argument that all women find great satisfaction from domestic roles. Her research stemmed from surveying fellow Smith College graduates before their twenty-year reunion and finding a deep lack of fulfillment in their lives. The women surveyed felt their sense of self was overshadowed by their roles as mothers and wives. Other feminists critiqued Friedan's call for women to work outside the home, as if the working-class and poor women had not already been doing work both inside and outside the home. Friedan idealized work outside the home and superimposed a negative connotation on work inside the home and the possibility of finding happiness in it. She also encouraged women to seek opportunities that would afford personal meaning and fulfillment, again neglecting the position of privilege one had to be in already to complete such a task. Her work, therefore, was said to show a limited understanding of economic and racial stratification. Friedan and almost thirty other women and men co-founded the National Organization of Women (NOW) in 1966, hoping to solidify "partici-

pation in the mainstream" (their token slogan). NOW, much like National Women's Studies Association, underwent serious problems with racism and homophobia in the years ahead.

An executive order in 1967 expanded affirmative action to include gender as a category through which one could be discriminated against. In 1969, Redstockings, a feminist group from New York City, decried patriarchy as the most basic form of domination and the one thread that ran through all other forms of oppression. In their manifesto they called for a revolution against patriarchy. Also in 1969 the Gay and Lesbian Rights movement was launched after the riots at Stonewall Inn in New York City. Patrons organized to resist and protest the ongoing police raids and harassment.

In 1971 *Ms. Magazine* appeared as an insert in *The New York Times*. The following year it was published on its own, and editors and journalists Letty Cottin Pogrebin and Gloria Steinem moved to the forefront of the women's movement. The magazine was the first of its kind, analyzing policy and custom and debunking tradition from a strong feminist perspective.

Title IX was passed in 1972, granting equal access to educational programs or activities receiving financial assistance in higher education. In other words, educational institutions cannot discriminate on the basis of gender for any admissions, recruitment, course offering, financial aid, housing, benefits, scholarships, athletics, or any other activity or program. The following year saw another major legal milestone: *Roe v. Wade* established a woman's right to a safe and legal abortion in the first trimester of pregnancy and allowed for individual states to set regulations on abortions in the second trimester. This is one of the most significant Supreme Court decisions of the twentieth century, inciting both great support and opposition during the three decades since the initial ruling. Concerns that the decision may be overturned are always present. The governor of South Dakota signed a ban on abortions

in early 2006, and pro-choice organizations called for other states to follow suit.

During the 1970s women established many community organizations, bookstores, clinics, child care centers, shelters, and other establishments to build awareness and coalitions. Coalitions were difficult to build because of the variety of ideologies that cut across the movement. Nevertheless, in late summer of 1970 thousands of American women went on strike to protest inequality, demand equal opportunities, and remember the fiftieth anniversary of women's suffrage. Mainly in large cities, women took to the streets with what became endemic slogans of the time. Feminism resurged in popular consciousness with a vengeance. With greater access to birth control, women also felt they had greater control of their reproductive health. Women were realizing how political the personal was and the importance of consciousness raising. Political awareness and consciousness raising became strategies for education and empowerment. The family, workplace, and other public and private spheres were transformed as a result of the history of the women's movement. Women continued to fight to define and redefine their own sexuality outside of the heterosexual matrix as well as within. Some feared diverse interests would further threaten and fragment feminism, regarding it as a singular movement focused specifically on gender, on women, and not on identity as it is lived in the intersection of politics, desires, and experiences.

Shirley Chisholm, Bella Abzug, Betty Friedan, Myrlie Evers, and Gloria Steinem founded the National Women's Political Caucus in 1971. Chisholm was the first black woman elected to Congress (in 1964) and the first to run for president in the Democratic primaries. Women continued to understand the need to hold political office as one way to change rights and access. Between 1970 and 1973 the Cómision Femenil Mexicana Nacional and the Chicana Service Action Center were formed to address the multitude of issues facing Mexican and Chicana women, one of which was mandatory ster-

ilization. They gained the right to create bilingual consent forms and a seventy-two-hour waiting period before consent. In 1974 the Coalition of Labor Union Women (CLUW) came together, representing more than fifty trade unions, to improve the status and working conditions of women workers. CLUW continues to work toward affirmative action, union organization, and increasing women's roles in legislation and politics.

In 1975, *Signs: Women, Culture, and Society,* a journal for new feminist scholarship, was first published. By 1976 domestic violence was another area of great struggle for legislation; the Domestic Violence Act afforded more comprehensive protection than had been available previously for victims of domestic violence. The First National Woman's Conference met in 1977, chaired by Bella Abzug, and exposed the wide differences between opposing ideas on the Equal Rights Amendment. The amendment fell short of ratification again in 1982. In 1978, more than 100,000 people marched in Washington DC to support ratification of the amendment, and in 1979 the first national march for gay and lesbian rights took place in Washington, DC. Catharine MacKinnon and Andrea Dworkin worked to bring awareness of the link between sexual harassment, pornography, and civil rights. MacKinnon wrote *Sexual Harassment of Working Women: A Case of Sex Discrimination* and *Only Words,* and Dworkin wrote *Woman Hating, Pornography: Men Possessing Women, Right Wing Women, Intercourse,* and *Heartbreak: The Political Memoir of a Feminist Militant.*

The 1980s were characterized by strong conservative politics and reactions to ensuing censorship. AIDS came to the forefront of public concern. In 1981, Gloria Anzaldúa and Cherríe Moraga edited *This Bridge Called My Back: Writings by Radical Women of Color;* Alison Kim, Cristy Chung, and A. Kaweah Lemeshewsky edited *Between the Lines: A Pacific/ Asian Lesbian Anthology;* and Gloria Hull edited *Women Are White, All the Blacks Are Men, But Some of Us Are Brave: Black Women's Studies*—all groundbreaking anthologies meant to rupture both the

heteronormativity and whiteness pervasive in feminist writing thus far. Works such as these, as well as the many community organizations that followed, changed how we define identity and what work needed to be done for greater public awareness and acceptance. Students and faculty around the nation were continuing to fight for the university to be a space for inclusion with the growth of women's studies, black studies/African American studies, Latino studies, Asian/Asian American studies, queer studies, and other ethnic and political studies programs. Students and faculty demanded greater diversity and action in their studies and sought to increase the training ground for future activists.

The 1980s saw World Conferences on Women hosted in Denmark and Kenya. President Carter instituted the first National Women's History Week, but it was not until 1987 that Congress changed this to a month and designated March as Women's History Month. In 1984 Walter Mondale and Geraldine Ferraro teamed up as presidential and vice-presidential candidates, making Ferraro the first woman to run for vice president. Wilma Pearl Mankiller was elected first woman principal chief of the Cherokee Nation in Oklahoma. In 1987 the second National Gay and Lesbian Rights march drew five times the attendance of the 1979 march. In 1988, despite President Regan's previous veto, congress passes the Civil Rights Restoration Act, which reinstated full coverage of Title IX provisions. In 1989 Felice Schwartz wrote an article for the *Harvard Business Review* titled "Mommy Track," and although she stated it was more expensive for companies to hire women (for which she received much criticism), she stressed the need for institutionalized programs to address the needs of parents, both women and men. Schwartz wanted women's talents to be recognized not ignored. Political correctness wars weighed heavily on all aspects of social life, and a backlash was pending. There was a shift from social politics and consciousness to individual merits and accolades. Many declared the end of feminism, the start of a postfeminist era, and a separation between

feminist ideas and calling oneself a feminist, creating an anti-feminist climate.

Conservative politics continued into the early 1990s, with two Republican presidents completing three terms in succession and a Democrat being sworn in by mid-decade. In 1990 President Bush signed legislation for the government to collect data on hate crimes, excluding gender as a motivator for such crimes. President Clinton later amended the legislation to include gender as another motivation for hate crimes. Robert Bly, the famous novelist, wrote *Iron John: A Book About Men* in 1990, in which he used essentialist arguments about manhood similar to those of radical and cultural feminists. The book is said to have been the catalyst for the **mythopoetic** men's movement. R. W. Connell wrote a response, *Masculinities,* in 1995, discussing the wide array of masculinities that lived throughout the world. In 1992 more than 700,000 people came together for a pro-choice rally in , DC, the March for Women's Lives. Susan Faludi wrote *Backlash: The Undeclared War against American Women* in 1992, discussing the ways in which society reacted to the progress of feminism. *Ms. Magazine* resurfaced as a bimonthly publication, and "girl power" infused popular culture. Toni Morrison won the Nobel Prize for Literature. In 1994 the Violence against Women Act was passed by Congress, extending funding for state programs to create crisis centers, hotlines, and shelters. The Gender Equity in Education Act was also passed in 1994. A second Violence against Women Act was passed in 1998 to extend funding to sexual assault programs. Rebecca Walker edited *To Be Real: Telling the Truth and Changing the Face of Feminism* in 1995, noting the changing scope of feminism toward the end of the twentieth century.

The third wave of feminism was well under way, challenging the essentialism that tended to motivate second-wave discussions. Texts on the body were being published, emphasizing the need to address the corporal in various ways; among the many are *Unbearable Weight: Feminism, Western Culture and the Body; Space, Time and Perversion: Essays on the Politics*

Mythopoetic

using myth, poetry, folklore, fairytales, and archetypes to gain personal insight into (in this context) gender roles, masculinity, femininity, and well-being

of Bodies; and *Volatile Bodies: Toward a Corporeal Feminism*. Post-structuralism helped infuse feminism with a clearer analysis of power and representation to alter monolithic interpretations of gender and identity. Popular culture became a rich terrain for deeper investigations into representations, stereotypes, and culture. Dichotomies or binaries of identity gave way to hybrid understandings of lived experience and a retooling of language to capture the nuances of lived experience. Heywood and Drake (1997) state, "Third wave feminism, feminism in Generation X, is not 'power feminism.' It's not about trying to be men or women either. It's about trying to think through what 'coalition' might mean and on what basis a 'community' might really come into being" (p. 50). Third-wave feminism also crossed gender borders and tried to leave the existing binaries of gender behind, redefining where feminist thinking and practice originates and lives. Third-wave feminists continue the critique of femininity while paying closer attention to the construction of desire and pleasure as mechanisms for feminist activism.

2000s

By the early 2000s, there were 700 women's studies, feminist studies, or gender studies programs around the nation offering undergraduate degrees, minors, graduate certificates, and graduate degrees. A number of anthologies and edited books by young, diverse feminists made their mark on feminist thinking and practice. Among these are *Colonize This! Young Women of Color on Today's Feminism*; *Manifesta: Young Women, Feminism, and the Future*; *Listen Up: Voices from the Next Feminist Generation*; *Catching a Wave: Reclaiming Feminism for the 21st Century*; *The Fire This Time: Young Activists and the New Feminism*; *Grassroots: A Field Guide for Feminist Activism*; and *We Don't Need Another Wave: Dispatches from the Next Generation of Feminists*. The Internet also opened a critical space for the exchange of ideas and events, providing multiple perspectives at the click of a mouse or a touchpad. The 2000s pushed for wider

understanding of feminism through gender studies, queer theory, and transnational studies, with a plethora of literature on these discourses such as *Transnational America: Feminisms, Diasporas, Neoliberalisms (Next Wave: New Directions in Women's Studies); Scattered Hegemonies: Postmodernity and Transnational Feminist Practices* (this one was published in the 1990s); *Feminism without Borders: Decolonizing Theory, Practicing Solidarity; Methodology of the Oppressed;* and *Queer Theory, Gender Theory: An Instant Primer.* In 2000 several important marches took place: the Millennium March on Washington, DC for lesbian, gay, bisexual, and transgender rights; the World March of Women 2000, where activists on five continents organized and marched to draw attention to global issues that affect women's lives; the Million Mom March against gun violence; and Brides March Against Domestic Violence, where women in wedding dresses marched to raise awareness.

On September 11, 2001, the nation was devastated by terrorist attacks in New York, Virginia, and Pennsylvania. Attempts at securing national borders endangered individual liberties and civil rights as a surge of patriotism swept the nation and troubling discussions about who is and can be an American were revisited, harking back to decades past.

By mid-decade the March for Women's Lives drew more than 1 million protestors to Washington, DC for the right to choose. In 2005 there was the March to Protest Femicide on the U.S./Mexico border, in which NOW introduced its campaign in a press conference and marched across the border to Mexico in protest of the unsolved murders of Juarez women (http://www.now.org/issues/global/juarez/12–13–05juarez.html).

Massachusetts legalized civil unions in the fall of 2005. In 2006 the House of Representatives renewed the Voting Acts Right of 1965, renaming it the Fannie Lou Hammer, Rosa Parks, and Coretta Scott King Voting Rights Act Reauthorization and Amendments Act of 2006. It was renamed to honor these women, who fought selflessly for everyone's

right to vote without exclusion, taxes, or literacy tests. A global women's summit took place in Egypt to build transnational alliances to advance women's economic development. The HPV (human papillomavirus) vaccine was approved by the U.S. Food and Drug Administration, and the nation debated whether vaccination should be mandatory for young women. In 2007 Nancy Pelosi was made the first woman Speaker of the House. Dr. Drew Gilpin Faust was elected as Harvard University's first woman president. In the latter half of 2007 the Iraq war continues, extending already long tours for women and men soldiers without a decision to retrieve troops in sight. At the time of writing, Hillary Rodham Clinton and Barack Obama are running for the Democratic presidential nomination. In the face of a generally conservative national climate, feminist thinking and activism persists to secure equity and egalitarianism in multiple private and public spheres for all who continue to be disenfranchised by capitalism and corrupt democratic practices.

■ ■ ■

This overview of feminist individuals, groups, publications, lectures, policies, and events is evidence of how necessary networking, collaborating, organizing, conversing, and inquisitive minds are to theorizing. The collection here is neither exhaustive nor entirely inclusive, of course; I give you a sampling of the continuity of feminist activity over the centuries. Note how basic ideas instigated speeches and writings, often rupturing the public sphere, its norms, and its expectations and bringing speakers and activists who incurred significant personal sacrifice under great scrutiny. Speeches, writings, and actions started in critical reflections on daily rituals or habits. Many activists endured a split between private and public life, weathering the turbulence of both, making controversial ideas public and enacting these even within traditional gender roles. None of these individuals followed solitary or

heroic paths; they accomplished social change through deep friendships and alliances. We cannot ignore the context of these changes, the sociopolitical times, and technological advances facilitating distribution and community organizing. I focus on this trajectory of ideas and activism to situate academic theorizing and to highlight letter writing, publishing, public speaking, policy drafting, petitioning, and dialoguing as essential groundwork. I am not interested in marking one point of origin in feminist theory. There are many beginnings, and feminist theories emerged little by little, through several works, correspondence, and actions that were later published or discussed in publications that set the foundation for a discipline. Keeping this rich history in mind, recognize the importance of theorizing as a sustainable daily action, one that capitalizes on the **liminal spaces** of existence and propels new ways of being.

> **Liminal spaces**
> gaps created by the juxtaposition of binary terms; the gaps in between the extreme positions on any continuum

What Do We Do with Theory?

Theory is a comprehensive explanation of any phenomenon or of the relationship between phenomena that facilitates more profound understanding of any condition. Theory can provide a set of principles to organize one's thinking and actions. In other words, theory provides keys to analysis and further inquiry in solidifying or challenging one's mission or project. Theory often affords a certain way of thinking that helps to frame the world, self, and others. Davis, Sumara, and Luce-Kapler (2000) state:

> Derived from the Greek *theorein,* to gaze upon, the term *theory* refers to ways of seeing things. A theory is a system of interpretation that both helps us to make sense of experiences and, in turn, that focuses attention on particular events (while pushing others in into. (p. 52)

Feminist theories do this by exposing gender inequity, politics, and rights, helping us to rethink interpersonal and intrapersonal relationships of power. The danger of some feminist theorizing is

that it may further essentialize gender, sex, roles, femininity, or masculinity, among many other issues that fall within the scope of feminism. Feminist theory cuts across numerous ideologies and disciplines, recognizing a wide range of subject positions and connections. Comprehending these ideologies and paradigms allows us to ask more accurate questions.

A constant thread throughout the history outlined above is the ability of people to organize on the basis of key, well-analyzed, well-articulated ideas. Each one of the individuals mentioned took the time to observe patterns in society, human behavior, and their own lived experiences to create compelling arguments for change. This is the purpose of theory, to push our thinking, behavior, and actions to deeper critical awareness and understanding of self and others, in particular provoking our imagination to enact what is not yet. In this way, theory becomes **proleptic;** it creates a kaleidoscope of possibilities and provides potential tools for change.

Proleptic

the potential of the future recognized in the present, the not-yet

Heuristics

a method for discovering knowledge through experimentation, analysis, and problem solving

Theory allows us to investigate the ways in which to read feminism; it gives us the tools to recognize natural and constructed phenomena as potential **heuristics.** Most times we distrust theory—we deem it abstract and vehemently contend that it is disconnected from practice, from reality. Many believe they are not smart enough to read theory, to tear it apart until understanding comes through in intelligible ways. We are conditioned to fragment our world, to separate the why from the what and the how, and often we think that to pull these fragments together is an overwhelming feat (see Chapter Five). It is not. The struggle many times is not in comprehending theory, but in undoing the perceptions with which we have grown too familiar. How we read the world and with what veracity we approach the world determines our relationship to knowledge production and activism.

We have also grown to distrust theory because it seems not to resonate with who we are, not to represent multiple subjectivities. One of the many critiques of feminist theory is that in its attempt to

bring attention to the inequities afflicting women, it by default attempts to essentialize what "woman" is and to exclude how gender is lived not just by women. In the project to secure recognition, many times decisions must be made about the parameters by which to recognize, simultaneously creating exclusions (see Chapter Four). No one theory will ever be useful in isolation; rather, our breadth of knowledge affords critical discernment of which ideas to juxtapose or combine for praxis. Many see theory as too complex and wish for simpler explanations. This is often a reactionary stance to the responsibility then placed on us to situate ourselves in any theoretical or pragmatic discussion.

Others wonder where feminist theory came from, and Grant (1993) proposes feminist theory is

> a history of ideas . . . invented in the midst of a struggle . . . radical women realized that the Left, for whatever reasons, could not incorporate politics relating to problems of sexism . . . feminists began to write their own new ideas on the subject . . . feminist theory was invented in the course of this conversation between feminism and the Left . . . One reason why radical feminists became the primary builders of feminist theory is simply that the academic roots and intellectual nature of the New Left meant that the women who came out of that tradition were predisposed to consider theory as essential to politics. (pp. 17–18)

Inherent in the paradigm shift from modernism to postmodernism is the political impetus behind knowing and different methods for education. Feminist theories, in particular, articulate the urgent need for political education, where using and producing knowledge is a political act. To unite the personal and political, the private and public, the self and other, demands deep contemplation and analysis of the ways in which norms are constructed and protected for the benefit of a few. There is no doubt that living one's politics is difficult and being aware of one's subjectivity and public responsibility can be daunting, but keeping the necessity of struggle at bay does not begin to address social and individual inequity.

Next I want to explore briefly the ways in which feminist theory split into theories, at last acknowledging the **intersectionality** of gendered lives.

Feminist Theories

Intersectionality

the way sexism, racism, classism, ageism (and any -ism) intersect in lived experience, bringing awareness to the varying degrees of oppression in layered structures of power

Feminist theory was rightly challenged to address more accurately the intersections of race, ethnicity, gender, class, sexual orientation, geography, language, ability, and a multitude of other social factors and roles. Unfortunately, the residue of a monolithic feminist politics still plagues the field. The tendency to see only gender or racial or economic injustice is undeniable, yet we cannot keep dividing ourselves into discrete categories, because the essence of one always leaks into another. The theories discussed below start us off on the right track as they force richer (and far more complex) feminist perspectives, mainly around issues of race, ethnicity, and sexual orientation. Critical race theory and queer theory are often credited with providing frameworks for pluralization. These splits (race and sexuality) are not without limitation; in fact, they often produce more exclusions. Nonetheless, the goal is to follow where we have been, to explore these contributions as springboards for further work in a postmodern intertextual feminist politics. These are beginnings. In addition, take into account how various feminist perspectives advocated for differing degrees of separation from mainstream feminism, with little interest in building coalitions. Both intentions (separating and building coalitions) are vital to feminist theorizing and understanding across constructed borders.

Black Feminist Thought and Womanist Feminism

Black feminist thought questions normative blind spots that essentialized gender and silenced race, ethnicity, and class. Sweeping descriptions of gender discrimination seldom delved into the intersections of gender and race as it was lived over time. Black feminists poignantly raised a collective con-

sciousness about race and class. As Sherri Barnes (2007) concisely states:

> Contemporary black American feminists have identified the central themes in black feminism as evidenced in over a century of struggle in the U.S. These include: 1) the presentation of an alternative social construct for now and the future based on African American women's lived experiences, 2) a commitment to fighting against race and gender inequality across differences of class, age, sexual orientation, and ethnicity, 3) recognition of black women's legacy of struggle, 4) the promotion of black female empowerment through voice, visibility and self definition, and 5) a belief in the interdependence of thought and action.

In response to sexism and racism, in between the women's movement and the black liberation movement, black feminist thought and womanism gave voice to the limitations and shortcomings of these movements and demanded the equity espoused in public rhetoric. Frustrated by the racism and sexism displayed by those professing to have transcended these issues through social action, black feminists emerged as catalysts for fundamental shifts in how we understood oppression and injustice. Not caving in to the pressures to singularize feminism, many advocated for separatist practices, whereas others sought to build bridges across differences. Regardless of intent or outcome, race is inseparable from the ways we live gender; black feminist and womanist feminism are pivotal in critically articulating this. Commonly cited authors in black feminist thought are Angela Davis, Patricia Hill Collins, Barbara Christian, Beverly Guy-Sheftall, Kimberle Crenshaw, bell hooks, Ann duCille, Joy James, Valerie Smith, Hortense Spillers, and Wahneema Lubiano. The term "womanist" is mostly credited to Alice Walker, and its intention is to mark a separation from the feminist movement in charting new territory for black feminism through more poetic expressions and closer links to African culture and heritage. Key writers in this area are Alice Walker, Audre Lorde, Hazel Carby, Shirley Anne

Williams, Elsa Barkley Brown, Marcia Riggs, Dolores Williams, and Emilie Townes.

Latina/Chicana Feminism

Latina/Chicana feminism (*Xicanisma,* to use Ana Castillo's term) raises issues not only of race but of ethnicity, language, geography, migration, religion, and class as they traverse gender and culture. Latina feminist discourses contend that identity is not defined by any one social marker of identity and that it is at the intersection of gender, race, ethnicity, language, and sexuality that resistance to colonialism and nationalism occurs. Latina feminism is an ongoing cultural production situated across the United States as different ethnicities add to the multiple definitions of Latina (Cuban, Puerto Rican, Mexican, Dominican, Venezuelan, Colombian, Nicaraguan, etc.). Each nationality discusses various political issues most relevant to its geography, history, and culture. This is further complicated by migration and hyphens as younger generations stretch the conversations into new phases of Americanization. Elizabeth Garcia outlines the following as tenets/goals for Latina feminism:

- That our oppression is not just as women, but that we also struggle against injustices based on race, class, sexuality, age, and disability.
- We recognize and adamantly proclaim that our struggle is not against men, but against Patriarchy. We therefore welcome Latino and non-Latino men as an integral part in our feminist movement.
- Through our various forms of activism we address issues that affect Latinas' every day lives including: pay equity, reproductive rights, health care, and education. These issues, however are addressed from our particular cultural perspectives and historical contexts.
- We stand in solidarity with other women of color and their movements for equality and social justice.
- We believe in building coalitions with *all* women on a basis of mutual respect and equality. (http://www.latinafeminist.com)

Chicana feminism speaks directly to inequity lived by Mexican American and Chicana women, using various social theories to politicize cultural, social, political, economic, and migratory roles and experiences while attempting to bridge many contradictions. Chicana feminism often resonates with other Latina experiences; the borders of discourse and nationality are ultimately porous. Latina feminism overall is grounded in a *mestiza* genealogy and history. Key authors to read are Gloria Anzaldúa, Emma Pérez, Ana Castillo, Chela Sandoval, Cherrie Moraga, Norma Alarcón, Antonia Darder, Pat Mora, Maria Lugones, Sandra Cisneros, Dolores Delgado Bernal, Norma Cantú, Aurora Levins Morales, Ruth Behar, Isabel Moya, Carolina Aguiar, Norma Vasallo, Aida Hurtado, Anna Nieto Gomez, Martha Cotero, Lynn Stonner, Alma Garcia, Gabriela Arredondo, Rosa Linda Fregoso, and many others.

Native American/Indigenous Feminism

Native American feminism addresses the ways mainstream feminism has neglected the most obscene form of colonialism on North American soil. The disenfranchisement of numerous tribes and indigenous people on the mainland, Hawaii, and Alaska is at the center of Native American and indigenous feminist discourses. Among the first priorities is reclaiming the rights of indigenous people. The Indigenous Women's Network, established in 1985, contends the inherent rights are

1. our right to self determine our social, political and economic status
2. the recognition and respect to our ancestral lands and territories
3. the recovery of traditional health care practices and access to health care
4. intellectual and cultural property rights and the right to control the biological diversity of our territories. (http://www.indigenouswomen.org/aboutus2.htm)

There is a concerted effort to reconnect to native languages and customs while re-energizing agency,

empowerment, and leadership and fighting gender discrimination, racism, and environmental racism. According to Schulz (2001), Native American women resisted on two fronts: first in their oppression as tribal people, and second on a cultural front in the reorganizing of power in the tribes as a result of externally imposed patriarchy. Key authors to read are Sarah Winnemucca, Paula Gunn Allen, Janet McCloud, Ramona Bennett, Kathleen Donovan, Ruth Behar, Deborah Gordon, Julia Emberly, Wilma Mankiller, Sandy Grande, Madonna Thunderhawk, Hunkpapa Lakota, Phyllis Young, Sally Roesch Wagner, Amanda J. Cobb, Janet Spector, Kate Shanley, Pam Colorado, M. A. Jaimes Guerrero, Angela Gonzales, Judy Kertesz, Carol Lee Sanchez, Winona LaDuke, Grace Thorpe, Leslie Marmon Silko, Anna Lee Walters, Clara Sue Kidwell, and Janet Campbell Hale.

Asian American Feminism

Asian American feminism, similar to other discourses, is a political hybrid linking very different cultures, beliefs, languages, religions, and customs (Shah, 1997). It attempts to undermine patriarchy, sexism, and racism in both Asian and American culture. Much is written about the co-opting of the Asian American woman for market value and consumption; resisting all-too-common stereotypes of submission and model minorities, these cultural impositions are experienced from multiple vantage points. A critical turn in Asian American feminism is the precise theorizing of colonialism and postcolonialism, particularly the criticism of capitalism and imperialism. Equally critical of global attempts to merge East and West, Asian American feminists alert us of the dangers once again of the co-option, appropriation, and unequal power relations of these endeavors. The effects are severe and expansive, much like the previous theorizations of feminism. Asian American feminism is widely diverse despite the monolithic overlay of mainstream media and literature. Shah (1997) proposes:

There is no political point in just talking about Asian American women's experiences, even as the very question rests upon the years of vital scholarship and creative work done on detailing that experience. What it makes political sense to talk about is how the forces of racism, patriarchy, and imperialism specifically affect Asian American women. And, most importantly, how Asian American women counter resistance to those forces. In other words, about a racially conscious, international feminism: Asian American feminism. (pp. xiii–xiv)

What Shah contends is closer to a pan-Asian political consciousness advocating for gender equity across cultural and geographic differences. Some key authors are Uma Narayan, Esther Ngan-ling Chow, Sonia Shah, Gayatri Chakravorty Spivak, Chandra Mohanty, Inderpal Grewal, Shin Ja Um, Phillipa Kafka, Gia B. Lee, Ailee Moon, Young I. Song, Yen Le Espiritu, Purvi Shah, Margaret Abraham, Jean Lau Chin, Margaret Chin, Phoebe Eng, Shirley Hune, Gail M. Nomura, Laura Hyun Yi Kang, Margaret Kimura, Pooja Makhijani, Vickie Na, Lynn Lu, and Rachel Lee.

Islamic Feminism

Islamic feminism advocates equal gender rights and social justice within an Islamic cultural matrix dating as far back as the seventh century. It was considered radical then, as it is now, for interrupting patriarchal customs. Bardran (2006) explains:

Islamic feminism has taken on the two-fold task to expose and eradicate patriarchal ideas and practices glossed as Islamic—"naturalised" and perpetuated in that guise—and to recuperate Islam's core idea of gender equality (indivisible from human equality). For this Islamic feminism has incurred enemies from within and without the Muslim community: 1) from within—men who fear the loss of patriarchal privilege and women who fear the loss of patriarchal protection, and 2) from without—those whose pleasure and politics are found in denigrating Islam as irredeemably anti-women.

The new Islamic feminist paradigm began to surface a decade and a half ago simultaneously in old Muslim societies in parts of Africa and Asia and in newer communities in Europe and North America.

For some, the intersection of Islam and feminism may seem incongruous; yet, as Badran and others contend, Islamic feminism is grounded in an ethic of equity in both public and private spheres based on the Qur'an. Despite this, much contention exists between the interpretations of theory/ideology/values and practice/rituals. These gaps are mediated by a wealth of competing visions for the future of Islamic countries and their peoples. Historically, women had central roles as advisors and generals in the army, but as societies moved away from the Qur'an or formed wider interpretations of its text, equitable practices changed dramatically; hierarchical exercises of power were commonplace and women were relegated to subservient roles. A wide range of literature exists that discusses practices of resistance and agency, veiling practices, and women's and girls' access to education and work and provides critical commentaries on culture, religion, and patriarchy. What seems most salient in these discussions is the recognition of the ways in which religious texts have been open for varied interpretations, as well as appropriation, and how these are utilized as fact mostly for oppressive practices. Through postcolonial lenses current feminist work carefully examines policy, culture, and religion for activist reform and emancipation under current systems of law. Key authors to read are Leila Ahmed, Margot Badran, Asma Barlas, Nawal El Saadawi, Fatima Mernissi, Azizah al-Hibri, Riffat Hasan, Amina Wadud, Khaled Abou el-Fadl, Elizabeth Warnock Fernea, Cheryl Benard, Shaheen Sardar Ali, Nayereh Tohidi, Paula Homes Eber, Amina Wadud, Masha Shekarloo, Halima Krausen, Aditiana Dewi Erdani, Katajun Amirpur, Lily Zakiyah Munir, and many others.

Lesbian Feminism

Lesbian feminism builds on radical feminism (refer back to Chapter One) and purports that the liberation of women rests on being entirely woman-identified. Denouncing heterosexuality as oppressive and irreparable, lesbian feminism believes "the woman-identified woman commits herself to other women for political, emotional, physical, and economic support [above all else]" (Bunch, 1993, p. 174). In the strong belief that women are inherently more caring and loving, women are regarded as superior and men are considered as sole abusers of authority and power. Said to be a separatist and essentialist endeavor, lesbian feminism provides an important contrast to accepted definitions of "woman," rejecting any heterosexual construction or aesthetic. At times the standpoints of lesbian feminism are provocatively radical, as when Wittig (1980) emphatically states, "Lesbians are not women" (p. 32), because to signify woman employs heterosexuality and a perpetuation of oppressive binaries. Sidestepping reactionary stances, one is then pushed to contemplate the intellectual, linguistic, and practical implications of such denial; unless one is forced to think this through, critical opportunities for dislocating heteronormativity are lost. Lesbian feminism intends to dismantle categorizations of gender and traditional structures of relations, yet the latter are often reinscribed, assuming same-sex relationships are immune to patriarchy. Bunch (1993) continues:

> The lesbian rejects male sexual/political domination; she defies his world, his social organization, his ideology, and his definition of her as inferior. Lesbianism puts women first while society declares the male supreme. Lesbianism threatens male supremacy at its core. When politically conscious and organized, it is central to destroying our sexist, racist, capitalist, imperialist system. (p. 174)

The dangers of claiming supremacy and falling prey to ideological blind spots are evident in this quotation. To invert the hierarchy of power does not minimize or erase its impact. It is important to understand the sexual exclusion from mainstream feminism and the gender discrimination from gay men experienced mainly during the 1970s that led to the standpoint articulated above. Nonetheless, many see a continuum from lesbian feminism to queer theory (see Chapter Three for more information on queer studies), as Alderson and Anderson (2000) illustrate:

> As a reappropriation of a term of abuse, "queer" has been used to valorize those forms of sexuality which are not merely resistant to the "norm" but which carry the potential to subvert the very grounds on which such normative judgments might be made in the first place by refusing or rendering incoherent homo/heterosexual and often at the same time masculine/feminine binarisms. (p. 2)

Queer theory encompasses lesbian, gay, bisexual, transsexual, and transgender studies and contests essentialist categories while pushing for post-structural theorizing of the subject. There are diverse voices within queer theory, many at odds over the prioritization of sexuality over gender. Sheila Jeffreys, Arlene Stein, and Jacquelyn Zita have been most vocal, arguing against the silencing of gender (but no other identity register such as race, ethnicity, or class) in the reframing of "queer" as white gay male. These dissenting perspectives extend both theorizing and activism in the search for **alterity,** critique, and justice. It is in part the point of listing these diverse yet limited ranges of voices to stress the assorted perspectives necessary continuously to decenter static categorizations of identity and lived experience. Key authors to read are Lillian Faderman, Riki Wilchins, Teresa de Lauretis, Lisa Duggan, Deborah Britzman, Judith Butler, Eve Sedgwick, Judith Halberstam, Shane Phelan, Ann Fausto-Sterling, Paul Burston, Colin Richardson, Sheila Jeffreys, Annamarie Jagose, Nikki Sullivan, Suzanne Pharr, Michel Foucault, E. Patrick Johnson, Ian Barnard, Mae G. Henderson, Brett Beemyn, David

Alterity

the state of being radically different; reading for difference not yet assimilated

L. Eng, Amy Goodloe, Michael Warner, Mickey Eliason, Stephan Valocchi, Robert Corber, John Hawley, Mark Hawthorne, Suparna Bhaskaran, Diane Richardson, Janice McLaughlin, Mark Casey, Karen Lovaas, John Elia, Gust Yep, and Arnaldo Cruz-Malave, among many others.

Feminist Studies of Men

Men quite consistently have been the object of study in feminism, mostly as a reaction to patriarchy and male privilege. Since the 1980s more attention has been paid to studying masculinity and the myriad identity politics men live. Lorber (2005) believes the focus of feminist studies of men is "different men's statuses in social hierarchies, their varying privileges and disadvantages . . . the dissection of men as a diverse gender and the calls for changing masculinity and divesting men of their patriarchal privilege" (p. 219). These she sees as necessary resistances against the current gender order. Feminist studies of men explore a range of issues, dealing with privilege, power, sexuality, psychology, violence, rights, sports, health, fatherhood, militarism, pornography, gender roles, and sexism. Feminist studies of men, men's studies, and masculinity studies (interchangeable terms in most literature before 2000; see Chapter Three for further discussion) have been held suspect by many and embraced by those who want to engage men's accountability in living gender equitably and, more important for men, to share in collective responsibilities to enact social, cultural, and political change. Adams and Savran (2002) add:

> masculinity studies is thus dedicated to analyzing what has often seemed to be an implicit fact, . . . that men have historically enjoyed more than their share of power, resources, and cultural authority. Focusing critical interrogations on men, patriarchy, and formations of masculinity, scholars in many disciplines have sought to denaturalize de Beauvoir's observation that "it goes without saying that he is a man," by demonstrating that masculinities are historically constructed, mutable,

and contingent, and analyzing their many widespread effects. (p. 2)

Major analyses in the discourse focus on how power and identity are performed through varying degrees of authority and privilege, sometimes automatically granted, and other times contested. How power and identity are institutionalized, perpetuated, exalted, unquestioned, challenged, and resisted provides the building blocks for critical awareness in studying masculinity. Significant attention is given to who has been sacrificed by monolithic representations of masculinities across racial, ethnic, gender, and sexual topographies, with hopes to map spaces for change in building coalitions across gender identities. Key authors to read are Judith Kegan Gardiner, Jeff Hearn, David Savran, Rachel Adams, Michael Kimmel, Fred Pfeil, Michael Awkward, Don Belton, Herman Beavers, Todd Boyd, Jeffrey Brown, Kenneth Chan, Ben Carrington, Keith Harris, Isaac Julien, Kobena Mercer, Khaula Murtadha-Watts, William Pinar, Marlon B. Ross, Robert Staples, Maurice Wallace, Judith Newton, Sergio de la Mora, R. W. Connell, Martin Summers, Michelle Wallace, bell hooks, Robyn Wiegman, Tom Digby, Tim Edwards, Jackson Katz, Stephen Whitehead, Frank Barrett, Michael Messner, and others.

Conclusion

These short introductions to major splinter groups in feminist theories are meant to encourage more thorough tracings of feminist ideas and work—not without contention, since every inclusion produces even more exclusion. The project of intellectual exposure is packed with contradictions and is always imperfect. I offer such brevity as a fruitful sound bite to encourage the student of feminisms (which should be anyone interested in these discourses, not just those actually enrolled as "students") to use this work as a teaser for further inquiry, research, and knowledge production. The reality of this type of inquiry is better suited to thematic structures and

wide-ranging questions that resist leaving stated categories intact or unproblematized. Positionality is both complex and shifting in the flux of daily negotiated contexts and roles; therefore, growing more tolerant of multiple intersections may afford greater creativity in cultural change. I say "may," since to believe that knowledge directly leads to action collapses the premise of this entire book. One can work diligently (and suspiciously) toward a more direct path from knowledge to action; many early works in critical theory and pedagogy touted the givenness of such a destination. The fact of the matter is that the chasm between knowledge and action is huge, and the responsibility always resides with the knower and her or his commitment, passion, intent, desire, and need to turn what is known into what is lived. Consider this process in your own work and in the work of the many notable figures discussed in this chapter.

GLOSSARY

Alterity—the state of being radically different; reading for difference not yet assimilated

Heteronormativity—the construction of heterosexuality as the pervasive norm in society, establishing a naturalization of sex and gender roles

Heuristics—a method for discovering knowledge through experimentation, analysis, and problem solving

Intersectionality—the way sexism, racism, classism, ageism (and any -ism) intersect in lived experience, bringing awareness to the varying degrees of oppression in layered structures of power

Liminal spaces—gaps created by the juxtaposition of binary terms; the gaps in between the extreme positions on any continuum

Mythopoetic—using myth, poetry, folklore, fairytales, and archetypes to gain personal insight into (in this context) gender roles, masculinity, femininity, and well-being

Otherization—the process of marginalizing difference, most times through negative stigmas and stereotypes

Proleptic—the potential of the future recognized in the present, the not-yet

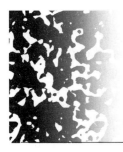

Contemporary Discourses

In the past three decades several discourses have stretched feminist theories in ways that have facilitated the emergence of new areas of research and restructured existing subcategories of study. As we surf various waves in feminism and typologies of feminist theory, recognition must be given to the disciplines that have come to bear heavily on the incomplete work of feminist thinking and politics. I say "incomplete" because discrimination does not target only one social category (gender), and we cannot disregard the complex politics of identity existing in our daily lived experience or the many issues consequently brought to public light (as stated in Chapter Two). The contemporary discourses specifically discussed in this chapter are gender studies, masculinity studies, queer studies, transnational studies, and visual studies. I then delve into other thought-provoking areas, such as body studies (including sports sociology), ecofeminism, and virtual gender/cyberfeminism, and end with a discussion of youth as docents and multi-ground sites of

activism and resistance. In discussing youth as docents, I recognize the guiding work they have already created in the popular press about feminism and future feminist theorizing. Capitalizing on possibilities for education writ large, I want to assert our larger public responsibility as educators, not just for those who are employed as such but for all those who recognize and understand they have the opportunity to teach by their mere presence. If we do not cultivate critical minds and actions in youth, I am afraid we will perpetuate our complicity in maintaining the status quo while undoubtedly allowing it to increase its incrtia. We need to question what we think we know through younger eyes, just as we have done through older (hopefully wiser) eyes. More spaces where youth find a place to create community and articulate their political voices are urgently needed. The contemporary discourses explored in this chapter set the stage for such work. The section on underground/multi-ground sites for resistance provides a brief overview of feminist collectives in the United States and other countries where we can learn more about how feminist theories are used in subversive ways. These uses can also provide models for unorthodox, creative directions for feminist theorizing.

This chapter is an attempt to familiarize you with each of the discourses of current cultural capital and to introduce you to central tenets, key authors, and discussions of how these complicate feminist theories and feminism in general. This is a chapter on **interdisciplinarity,** the ways in which multiple disciplines leak into one another and, as a result, create many useful or promising hybrids. The objective here is to focus on what these disciplines do intellectually and pragmatically. How might these disciplines bring forth new projects for more equitable living? What do we gain and sacrifice? What are the theoretical intersections that lead to different areas for inquiry? And how do we use these spaces for critical engagement in learning and social action? These are only a few of the pressing ques-

Interdisciplinarity

the involvement of two or more disciplines; an integration of concepts, ideas, and practices across disciplines for more holistic studies

tions raised as we move through the various discourses below.

Gender Studies

Gender studies is an integrated field studying gender, sexuality, and language in the cultural, social, health, political, and legal realms. The 1980s and 1990s marked the true arrival of gender studies in the literature and in academic circles. Much debate exists about the switch to "gender studies" from "women's studies" or the use of a compound programmatic title, such as "women's and gender studies." Many believe focusing on gender recentralized men and detracted from the necessary attention on women's issues. Others believe gender studies more aptly addressed the way we are all gendered through organizational practices, social systems, and relationships. As a separate discipline from women's studies or feminist studies, gender studies intends to be more inclusive, addressing a continuum of gender expressions and classifications. Realizing that gender affects men as well as women and any individual who defies mainstream categorizations of gender or sex, the literature problematizes gender as a social construction and more recently has stretched conceptions of gender and sex beyond the female/male binary. "Gender" is a politically contested term in and of itself, and "sex" has become an ongoing medical exploration as research provides evidence of common variations of XX and XY chromosomes, such as XXX, XXY, XXXY, XYY, XYYY, XYYYY, and XO (Kessler & McKenna, 1978; Lugg, 2007). Theorists in gender studies emphatically distinguish between gender and chromosomes, where the latter are no predictor of the former. Such research on gender and sex opens the door to discussions, understandings, negotiations, and acceptance of intersex, transsexual, and transgender sexual and gender identities. The schism created between sex, gender roles, and identities affords a rich space for **disidentification** from traditional scripts and restrictions on living a full and equitable life as defined by the person living it.

Disidentification
the questioning of and distancing from, in order to transform, traditional identification practices and culture

Gender, as a social and cultural construction with a certain accepted degree of arbitrariness, is often taken for granted unless it is set apart as female or femininity. Masculinity, as the barometer for gender, is usually considered a given. Until feminist critics highlighted these power differentials, differences were seen as natural and necessary. Thus began the struggle for equal representation, access, and rights. Gender, sex, and roles were written about, researched, and addressed privately and publicly, but it was not until the development of gender studies that the interchangeability of these terms decreased. Gender, as a term, took on a greater political tenor, manifesting a departure from highlighting a single point in a binary system. The field recognized power and difference as relational; consequently, the literature turned to encompass more complex theorizing on gender as a continuum of expression, representation, and lived experience. This is not to say that gender was discussed uniformly; ideology and philosophy still dictate what is said and questioned about gender, as well as how. Our perception of gender and how we relate it to what it means to be human prescribes the degree to which we are aware of our cultural and social conditioning. This awareness defines our commitment to gender equity and recognition of gender as either a binary or complex social category. We learn to see people, situations, experiences, artifacts, customs, and language as gendered. Gender is not only something that we inhabit but something we do and a façade we superimpose. Inherent in these constructions is what Pilcher and Whelehan (2004) offer as "gender order" from Jill Matthews's (1984) work on femininity; this is a hierarchy of privilege, a preference for one gender over another, instituting a deficiency mode that needs to be debunked. Pilcher and Whelehan state:

> The gender order is a patterned system of ideological and material practices, performed by individuals in a society, through which power relations between women and men are made, and remade, as meaningful. It is through the gender order of a

society that forms or codes of masculinities and femininities are created and recreated, and relations between them are organized. (p. 61)

These organized structures are not exactly benign or reciprocal, so it is crucial to perceive the direction of power and its target. Simply because gender codes are socially constructed does not mean they cannot be undone or redirected. The key word from the above quotation is "recreated": the codes can be carefully studied and reconstructed within a feminist politics. Gender studies helps us reconsider gender as relational, as delinked from biology; how we define gender depends on what it is not or what it is in contrast to. Feminist theories are shaken from their own gendered essentialism (which, of course, has been incredibly effective, but not sufficient; revisit the two scenarios I offered in Chapter One). Gender studies can provide access to a more holistic picture of gender construction and experience, as well as set the stage for ground-breaking and imaginative theorizing.

Masculinity Studies

The reexamination of gender led many to focus on masculinity and men's studies. Masculinity is the character or performance of being male exemplified through different social, political, historical, and cultural practices. It is pluralized (with the help of queer theory and critical race theory) to capture the various ways one can embody and express one's gender. Developing simultaneously with gender studies, masculinity studies strengthened in the 1980s and 1990s, presenting biological, scientific, mythic, and social explanations for masculinity. The intention of this subcategory (which has since become its own discipline) was to examine men and power among men in relation to women and others who identify as neither. Various subsections (men's studies, men's groups, men's movements, and masculinism) are associated with masculinity studies, but in reality these are politically quite distinct. Masculinism—one example that illustrates the most

essentialist tradition—was a countermovement to feminism with the specific intent to reclaim men's superiority and power and to address the anti-male sentiment in feminism dominant in the 1970s. The men's movement adopted several standpoints: masculinism, spiritual self-help and individual psychology, anti-sexism, pro-feminism, men's rights advocacy, and men's studies. Each of these is also informed by various politics, such as anti-patriarchal, progressive coalition, anti-feminist, and identity politics (Messner 2000). Men's studies often became the overarching term including all of the above with attention to the historical, political, social, and cultural constructions of being male.

Much as in the discussion of gender studies versus women's studies, masculinity studies (instead of men's studies) seems to be the preferred terminology in the current literature. Masculinity studies captures both the political intentions and diverse expressions and representations of being male, even when it is distinct from the genetic male body. Wiegman (2002) asks how we can "think about masculinity as a structure of identification in ways that could be wholly disconnected from genetic male bodies (if not fully from female ones)" (pp. 49–50). Masculinity studies serves as an important catalyst for unlearning patriarchy and restructuring gender privilege.

Before going too far into the discussion of masculinity studies, I would like to address a likely trepidation within feminist studies in regard to masculinity studies. A similar situation occurred within multiculturalism, African American studies, and Latino studies with the emergence of whiteness studies in the 1990s. Skepticism is a natural and healthy reaction (in my opinion, skepticism is always healthy regardless of how it was provoked) to the re-engagement of the dominant perspective or positionality, that is, whiteness and patriarchy. The reality is that whiteness and patriarchy never went anywhere; not to always contend with these is as dangerous as assuming they are the sole arbiters of power. If we continue to let the dominant "off the

hook," so to speak, we never engage in interrogating or debunking the power structures that sustain their dominance (which is similar to my argument in Chapter One). Although I understand the vehement resistance from some feminists, I lean toward active collaborations in reconstructing the limited parameters of discourse and performance within which we tend to box ourselves.

With that said, I would also like to draw some parallels between masculinity studies and the different waves in feminism. The first wave was about white men/white women (at least in popular culture). Through the second and third waves, there were modifications in the national organization, from it being about changing men to it being about men against sexism and homophobia. The new men's studies objective was to augment and support feminist scholarship. Between the original and new incarnations of men's studies there are two common ideological perspectives: first, pro-feminism—recognizing that men gain privilege from patriarchy and the oppression of women; second, non-feminism—maintaining that women benefit from the institutionalization of traditional gender roles and that such roles place men at a disadvantage relative to women. This latter ideological premise is the founding argument for masculinism. Masculinity studies, as the most current wave, sets itself somewhat apart from the aforementioned standpoints and adopts a less static angle for identity politics embracing a multifarious perspective on the study of masculinity.

Although I have not come across a reference to "waves" per se in the literature, many men critique masculinity studies for being as exclusionary as feminism was at the onset of both the movement and the academic area of study. Critiques center on token discussions of black and gay masculinities (much like early discussions about race and sexual orientation in feminism) and the paucity of discussions of other racial or ethnic identities or any identification outside straight versus queer. The rich intersections of race, ethnicity, sexuality, class, reli-

gion, power, and place within the construction of masculinity in private and public realms are too often glossed over, if they are recognized at all. To think that male privilege is embodied uniformly, or to think that patriarchy as a system of reproductive power does not affect and disadvantage men as well, sorely misses the importance of lived experience and compromises our intellectual contributions. The stoic man works as a performative for the stoic; it does not work if one is emotive, passionate, or caring, yet if one continues to believe men do not cry or emote other than in cool anger, for example, then this mode of being is restrictive and oppressive. Privilege is a fragile phenomenon, susceptible to the relationships between people and the context one is in. Of course, I am not denying larger social patterns of probability that dictate who is repeatedly afforded greater access, leniency, freedom, and so on more often than not. Do not get me wrong; it is quite evident where power resides. What I am suggesting is that the hold on power is not absolute, that the direction, intention, or use of power can change depending on context, that it can be temporal and in flux. Much like feminism or feminist studies, masculinity studies requires the constant evolution of theoretical frameworks.

Reading masculinity studies through a (politically progressive) feminist perspective or contemplating how masculinity studies expands feminist theories is an opportunity to discuss and understand gender in even more fluid ways, perhaps to understand masculinity as a performative act, a migratory one, containing a set of behaviors, mannerisms, and conceptual frameworks that are socially constructed and embodied not just by men, similar to femininity. These socialized practices are on a continuum of existence. I like what John MacInnes (1998) advocates as "gender vertigo" (borrowed from Connell [1995]), which I interpret as a willing decentering of what gender has been made out to be, feel like, and look like and what each of us has been made through it, including our response to gender. More specifically, gender vertigo can provide disidentifica-

tions as practices of freedom, as José Esteban Muñoz (1999) suggests. Both gender vertigo and disidentification can be used strategically as vehicles for destabilizing patriarchy and hegemony in masculinity studies and feminist theory. Alfredo Mirande (1997) alerts us to the ways that masculinity studies could also be and is being used as a strategy to undermine women's studies programs and to move toward a more generic (instead of inclusive) gender studies, to weaken feminist studies, or to reinscribe heterosexism. We absolutely should heed these tendencies, yet I think truly discussing gender in all its representations is as urgent as an interdisciplinary crossing of borders essential to intellectual and practical survival. Expanding feminist theories through masculinity studies or gender studies is but one way to critique static identity categorizations and power investments.

Queer Studies

Queer studies as a shifting discipline focuses on questioning normative practices, whether these are based on sexuality, gender, roles, identities, or behaviors. I use "shifting" because the nature of the discourse is to debunk categories, structures, and institutionalizations, so by its nature queer studies purposely remains fluid. Growing out of gay and lesbian studies, postmodernism, and post-structural theory, queer studies "has come to be associated with a new militancy in gay and lesbian [bisexual and transgender] politics—a determined push for visibility and a celebration of the **transgressive**" (Pilcher & Whelehan, 2004, p. 129). By use of the term "queer," the discipline aims to destabilize the accepted binaries of gender, identity, and sexuality and the assumption that the self is singular in identification or that it neatly follows a hierarchy of social factors (for instance, you might have heard people say that they are black first, then a woman/man, then gay/straight, etc.). How one enacts or conceptualizes the distance between these fragments of identity is a key tool in gauging our complicity

Transgressive

exceeding, advancing, or crossing a boundary or border of social expectation or acceptability

in what Judith Butler discusses as gender performance (which I would extend to identity performance), the ways we reproduce the norms by which we are signified (Pilcher & Whelehan, 2004). The smaller the space between these identifiers, the more likely we are to understand post-structural and queer theoretical implications for living. The term "queer" also becomes "an umbrella term for a coalition of culturally marginal sexual self-identification" (Jagose, 1996, p. 1). In queer studies, identity is a complex helix of interdependent and indeterminate social constructions. Thus, queer studies challenges the stable categories on which feminism was founded. For this reason, many question its merit and purpose, fearing it will undo centuries of political work and dismiss tangibly real ways in which identity categories affect daily living. For some, queer theorizing exemplifies the comforts academic contexts create for contesting these politics. Pouring out of these critiques is the shifting privilege of one identity space over another, the focus on fluid categories instead of static ones, the tendency to highlight the tension between street organizing and academic theorizing, and so forth. These juxtapositions are precisely the project of queer studies. In such artificial and constructed collisions, a wealth of resources and deeper understanding about the necessity of collapsing the walls between apparently competing entities manages to subsist. Queer studies offers new possibilities for theorizing the ontology of being and carving out spaces for hybridity, elasticity, and *mestizaje* (the practice of Anzaldúa's *mestiza* consciousness mentioned throughout this book), while simultaneously pushing for a rethinking of gender and sexual norms. I am not arguing for a devaluing of finite categories, but for a recognition of how porous these are, of the leaks that exist, and of the equally tangible slips into in-between resultant experiences that ultimately may transform how one looks back to where one is or where one started.

Queer theory is a tool of thought (Jagose, 1996) and as such provokes critically divergent reading practices. In essence, queer studies is about counter-narratives and counteractions where, just as Foucault points out, power is reproductive and in its presence there is always resistance, particularly in and through hegemonic contexts. Britzman (1998) inquires whether there is a queer pedagogy or whether we will continue to read straight as she pushes the reader to consider what queer theory might offer to the educational context. She states,

> I think of Queer Theory as provoking terms of engagement that work to recuperate . . . to exceed . . . contain and dismiss . . . Queer theory offers methods of critiques to mark the repetitions of normalcy as a structure and as a pedagogy . . . insist[ing on] the production of normalization as a problem of culture and of thought. (pp. 213–214)

Britzman offers three subcategories of analysis: the study of limits, the study of ignorances, and the study of reading practices. At the core of each is thinking or acting against the grain. The study of limits is "a problem of where thought stops, a problem of thinkability . . . [It] begins with the question, what makes something thinkable?" (p. 216). One must investigate what is dismissed or esteemed and for what reasons, as well as analyzing what one "cannot bear to know, what . . . must [be] shut out to think as it does" (p. 216). In the study of ignorances, ignorance is constructed in the lived spaces between theory, ideology, or belief system and practice, at the margins where idea and action are at odds and many times in contradiction. It is these spaces that need critical recognition and pedagogical exploitation. It is these spaces that hold potential for difference, these invisible and hypervisible moments of concrete examples where rhetoric breaks down and actions fall short. Here the politics of recognition that you will read about in Chapter Five get center stage as pedagogical texts/curricula for political work.

The final subcategory in Britzman's work is the study of reading practices. Using Shoshana Felman's analytic practices (practices of reading for alterity, practices of engaging in dialogue with the self as the

self reads, and practices of theorizing how one reads), Britzman (1998) offers a unique foundation for pedagogy. Reading for alterity requires readers to have a clear vision of who they are as a reader as they decode the words for difference. It is important to question who one is becoming through the reading process, as for Britzman reading can then serve as an interpretive performance where the self is distanced from what one claims as truth in the confrontation with the Other (in the text), and it is this space (as I mentioned earlier) that is conducive to transformative thinking or praxis. The second reading practice, the dialogue with the self, requires one to be aware of one's reactions as one reads, how one is responding to the author and the content, and what one accepts, argues against, instantly discredits, or derives inspiration from. The last reading practice establishes a different kind of distance, one in which the reader can develop her or his overall theory of reading, where a method for knowledge production is crystallized. This entire process, from the study of limits to the theory of reading, provides a unique experiential space for critical analysis and learning. I have turned this into an assignment for one of my graduate courses, and each time students find it incredibly transformative in shifting their thinking about themselves and reading and learning. Recently, per the suggestion of Jay Poole (a colleague from social work and a doctoral student), I added an article by G. D. Shlasko to be read in tandem with Britzman. Shlasko (2005), using Morris (1998) further explains queer theory and pedagogy and provides three approaches through which to define queer. The first, "queer as a subject position, describes people whose gender and/or sexuality fall outside of cultural norms and expectations . . . describing one's location relative to those norms" (p. 124). The second is that "as a politic, queer challenges the very idea of 'normal' . . . as both outside of gender and hetero-norms and also opposed to the existence of these norms and the structures that serve to police their boundaries" (p. 124). The third is that queer as an aesthetic "looks for and enjoys potentially subversive content in cultural texts of any media, from academic research papers to television advertisements to graffiti" (p. 124). These definitions are instructive in identifying the uses of queer analysis essential to a feminist politics. Queer studies presents itself as an essential theoretical element in the growth of feminist theories. It centralizes the need to expand how feminist theories are understood and enacted. For example, a discipline emerging out of the intersection between queer theory, feminist theory, and the history of sexuality is transgender studies, which focuses on transsexual and transgendered subjectivities through the navigation of everyday visibilities and invisibilities of repressive and hostile gender norms. Transgender studies is yet another example of the necessity continuously to interrogate the limits of thinkability and to theorize embodied fundamental assumptions about bodies, desire, gender, and identity (Namaste, 2000; Stryker & Whittle, 2006).

Transnational Studies

Transnational studies is a field exploring transnationalism (to connect and traverse national borders), its practices, intents, impacts, and range of perspectives about crossing political, cultural, economic, and religious borders. As a discipline it charts the effects of imperialism and colonialism and decentralizes the West as core axis. It is an interdisciplinary field that brings together the study of economic sustainability, human rights, gender rights, religious freedom, educational access, racial/ethnic rights, civil rights, social movements, nongovernmental organizations, grassroots activism, legal systems, and migration (displacements—voluntary and forced). Often postcolonial studies and transnational studies are grouped together, even though they diverge slightly in their projects and scope. Postcolonial studies examines the relationships between the British and French (as European superpowers) and the countries they colonized, as well as the subsequent development of Third World nations and

indigenous knowledge. This is not to imply that colonialism is a practice of the past; on the contrary, postcolonialism allows us to understand the lasting impact of living under colonial rule. Postcolonialism has contributed greatly to the ways we theorize about power and resistance, which has been extremely useful in shifting national conceptions of authority and privilege. Transnational studies can be used as a comprehensive term for postcolonialism, globalism, and internationalism. The larger intent is to make visible the other margins of mainstream feminism, that is, the global margins. Many fear that gender once again will be made less important than ethnicity, race, or religious beliefs as borders are expanded and traveled. Yet many others see the intersections of transnationalism or postcolonialism and feminism as a step toward a more informed analysis of difference, power, and resistance embodied through a new cartography of pluralism. In the context of international politics, gender is still important, as the power differentials between men and women compound the problems of poor living conditions (poverty, pollution, limited access to health care and education). Women, children, the elderly, and the sick bear the brunt of these continuing crises. In the transnational studies literature, "women" are a significant focus of study for the above reasons. Grewal and Kaplan (2000) add:

> Transnational feminist practices refer us to the interdisciplinary study of the relationships between women in diverse parts of the world. These relationships are uneven, often unequal, and complex. They emerge from women's diverse needs and agendas in many cultures and societies. Given a very heterogeneous and multifaceted world, how do we understand and teach about the condition of women? When we ask this question, relations between women become just as complicated as those between societies or between nations. Rather than simply use the model of information retrieval about a plurality of women around the world, a project that is both endless and arbitrary, we need to teach students how to think about gender in a world whose boundaries have changed.

Transnational studies and postcolonial theory widen the lens of the camera, so to speak, allowing information previously not considered or registered to occupy the foreground of the image. Unless we constantly problematize the familiar with the unfamiliar, a larger network of coalitions transgressing many borders and boundaries will not come to fruition.

The challenge here is to extend the current practices employed in the development of interdisciplinary fields to connect regions, geographies, nation-states, continents, and so on, with careful attention to the complex identity of each. Given increased technological progress, fluency, access, popularity, trade, and interaction, previous gaps in knowledge and distances collapse or implode, exposing the already disenfranchised to even more inequity and leaving them with minimal hypothetical possibilities for change. The exotic or unknown is further romanticized, and the privileged feel compelled to do something about their guilt. Transnational studies is as much about self as it is about other, insider, and outsider. Unless we are alert to the potential replication of these extremes, we are bound to export historical patterns of racism, xenophobia, sexism, classism, and exploitation (more so than we already have).

Much criticism has already been documented illustrating the resistance to Western feminism, particularly its imperialism and blindness. Freedom, awareness, critical consciousness, and empowerment are so narrowly defined that these notions have little applicability outside American national soil. Postcolonial theory acts as a pivotal tool of reflexivity to help us question the direction of power, who distributes it, who suffers at its hands, how it entangles everyone in complicity in the sustenance of existing hierarchies, and how to dispense with claims of truth. An entitlement to knowledge often extends a false and arrogant security about one's identity, which can prove disastrous in working through various communities of discourse or cultural/national borders. Feminism is not under the

sole purview of the West; women and men have struggled for equality and against subordination for centuries worldwide. Claims have been made to a universal sisterhood in the attempt to unite on the basis of an essential category of gender, but often such gestures do more harm than good since they subsume difference and gloss over harsh lived realities. The intentions are important; we need to step outside ourselves and reach out, but we also need to be open to being reached out to in ways we never imagined. We need to engage in what Mohanty (2003) calls "imagined communities" based on "potential alliances and collaborations across divisive boundaries" (p. 46) and developing horizontal comradeship, a notion that she attributes to Benedict Arnold. These collaborations and communities must surge from a reconstituted flow and seat of power if indeed we are invested in their success. In addition, any interactions must be contingent on reciprocity and mutual recognition.

What is the impact of transnational studies on feminist theories? Grewal and Kaplan (2000) offer this:

> For instance, as faculty in women's Studies we deal with, on the one hand, the ways in which feminist communities are being produced in cyberspace, and on the other hand, the new female industrial worker in multinational assembly lines, or the increasingly female population in prisons in metropolitan locations. Our challenge is to provide a framework in which to study all of these conditions together rather than ignoring one at the expense of the other. The study of transnational movements in relation to histories of colonialisms and postcoloniality will produce new feminist theories.

I also propose borrowing from gender studies and queer studies to widen what we consider studying and learning about as we travel theoretically, intellectually, and pragmatically into other landscapes to unlearn stereotypes about women and men, cultures, and religions across the globe.

Visual Studies

Visual studies, like the other disciplines discussed here, is an integrated discourse. It uses art history, media studies, literary theory, and cultural studies to interpret visual artifacts and language. Poststructuralism, semiotics, critical theory, and postcolonial theory are common analytical tools for the deconstruction and construction of image and text. Aside from the fact the discipline is a recurring research interest of mine, why would I request your focused attention on visual studies and what is the relationship to contemporary feminist theories? Let's see. The United States is a visual culture relying heavily on the relationship between image and text to convey both complex (policy, politics, government, human values) and simple ideas (products or services available, consumption, individual preferences). Given the pervasiveness of the visual in this culture, I propose we focus on the cultivation of responsibility, memory, and consciousness as we develop critical visual literacies through artistic/ aesthetic sensibilities and intellectualize/think about their impact on self and world, particularly how these perpetuate or reconstruct gender relations and possibilities for identity politics.

You might be hard-pressed to find arts education as part of the regular curriculum in K–12 schools unless you are in a magnet, charter, private, or alternative school. We can credit No Child Left Behind for the eradication of any subject that is not tested. The problem, then, is the juxtaposition of a society saturated with visual images and a citizenry ill-equipped to navigate such literacy. A visual culture demands a literate membership who can assess the significance of the images and text and thoughtfully act in productive ways not only as individuals but also as part of and for the collective (fellow human beings). Our schools are missing the opportunity to infuse a study of, and an active participation in, visual culture. In the curricular design of feminist studies, it is imperative for a component of that curriculum to be dedicated to visual literacy and the

development of the social responsibility of the creative thinker/student. The arts are both social and pedagogical. Because of this potential, it is crucial for students and theorists to have or develop a critical awareness of the implications and ramifications of the visual and textual in order to use visual literacy for social productivity (however small or large) and pedagogical understanding.

The arts have been censored and limited for centuries, as society saw only museums, galleries, and public spaces as appropriate places for this component of high culture. Current technology means that our culture is inundated with visual and textual designs from the minute we wake to the minute we go back to sleep. The formal aesthetic components of a work of art are now seen on billboards, magazine layouts, CD covers, iPods/mp3 players, cell phones, clothes, bus stops, benches, flyers, subway stations, stores, restaurants, the Internet, television, print . . . everywhere. Even though many may not see this as art (because it is commonly regarded as low art), they are continuously influenced and shaped by it. What they consume and define, as characteristic of who they are, is undoubtedly at least partially visual. So to recognize that our culture is undeniably visual is perhaps the first step; then it is equally important to read these visuals for information that prescribes what is desired, accepted, rejected, and perpetuated. As a result, it seems prudent that we develop a feminist awareness of our responsibility in reading, creating, and acting upon this visual culture.

Art is a social and political construction with an inherent intention to inform and communicate, even though it may appear merely decorative. Without understanding of the power of images, text, and visual culture, the opportunity to gain pedagogically and historically is lost. Images can often communicate across borders and disciplines to bridge otherwise disparate spaces. The accessibility of visual culture facilitates interventions into public spheres, where we can exercise our social responsibility, regardless of occupation or political commitments. Whoever creates any form of visual communication has a responsibility to consider implications and consequences once the artwork is publicized on any level, and whoever views it must have the skills to question and analyze what he or she is confronted with, as well as what he or she will do with it. Before this we need to have a grasp of the notion of a social consciousness, an understanding of realities beyond our own (a realization of the world's interconnectedness and our impact on the world), and a desire to cross limits established by the power structures of our own society and others. Once this consciousness is understood and dealt with, a self or social responsibility (ownership of the consequences of our actions) is more likely to develop. Feminist theories already require this, so when you direct an existing feminist consciousness to read visual culture, the results open up a plethora of texts and methods of knowledge production for feminist action and pedagogy. Reading visual culture for insights into cultural mores, public consciousness, **countercultural narratives,** market and nonmarket values, ideals, taboos, and numerous other matters provides concrete sites for critical feminist research. Carefully looking at and reading the foreground, middle ground, background, composition, colors, text, inclusions, exclusions, representations of beauty (by what is heralded and juxtaposed), and the locations and spaces of images tells a particular story about the culture and people of any geography. Every image is laced with theoretical constructs; feminist readers can be equipped to tease out both the explicit and the implicit meanings of visual culture (of race, gender, sexuality, and so on), readily using their environment as a resource for expanding and complicating feminist theories. Visual culture, generally speaking, positions the viewer in distinct ways to dictate what we make of what we see. Our gaze is our own conduit for agency; we construct our gaze as a result of our own perceptions of the world, subsequently debunking the unidirectional superhighway of consumption (Villaverde, 2006). I have previously said:

Countercultural narratives

perspectives resisting or subverting normative culture, society, or the status quo

The gaze, our look, how we engage by seeing is multidirectional and can both consume or reject, agree or disagree, condone or resist [as well as anything in between]. In actuality we have greater say so over what we choose to respond to, act upon, be involved with, care about, and look at. Our lives are so inundated by visual elements many times causing us to overlook all the information because we are simply overwhelmed. The pervasiveness of the visual does not automatically translate into accessibility creating the need to produce a way of knowing distinctive to the 21st century, one where the development of a visual literacy is prioritized, one that researches the obvious, implied, excluded, and possible. (pp. 569–570)

Feminist theories, then, have rich detours where theory and life are intrinsically linked through studies of visual culture. Visual culture becomes a substantial part of our socialization process. New communities are formed through these experiences, and learning is extended constantly beyond traditional spaces. This is not an entirely new area of study; *Signs: Journal of Women in Culture and Society* dedicated a special issue to visual cultures; Amelia Jones edited *The Feminism and Visual Culture Reader* and Ella Shohat edited *Talking Visions: Multicultural Feminism in a Transnational Age.* I included visual studies in this chapter with the intention of underscoring its utility in present and future feminist curricula and research. Jones (2003) maintains, "Both modes of thinking—feminism and visual culture—are, in this way, driven by political concerns and focus primarily on cultural forms as informing subjective experience" (p. 1). She subsequently adds, "[F]eminism is one of the ways in which we can most successfully come to an understanding of the image culture in which we are suspended" (p. 3).

Additional Thought-Provoking Grounds

There is so much to include, to research, to say. I have to keep reminding myself that this is a primer, an introduction, not an ever-evolving encyclopedia.

So to that end I want to mention (and I really mean mention, since this brief discussion will not do these subjects justice, but I hope it piques your interest) a few areas already within feminist theories that I think are indispensable, especially in our future theorizing and praxis. The body has been a zone of contention in feminism for centuries, a source of love/hate relationships with both self and others. I find the literature on body studies, sports and feminism, and sports sociology, its cultural and ethnic turns, its reconceptualization of strength, physicalness, and the possibility these provide for greater sense of personal and relational confidence genuinely necessary. In this zeroing in on the body, again we must look critically at aesthetics, its impact on how we distance ourselves from our bodies, how we connect to or live in them, what we do to them, and in the name of what (from decoration to reproductive technologies). The idea of rearticulating and recognizing various experiences and enactments of physicality so that it is not singularly defined as athletics seems to be a critical area of scholarship in terms of understanding the body (inclusive of the mind, of course) as a primary tool for interacting with the world. These areas of study would also extend our conceptions of desire, corporeality, movement, disability, health and well-being, visible inscriptions of ideology, work and labor, mutilation and torture, and numerous other issues situated in the body. Despite all that has been written on body studies, we vacillate between treating our own bodies as estranged family members and as temples of reverence (extreme comparisons, I know), and we continue to have disconnected, objectified, or solely utilitarian dispositions to our physicality. The continued study of the body, sports, and sociology may better prepare us to navigate the proliferation of technologies created to medicalize or pathologize our bodies.

Ecofeminism, an intriguingly complex field, forces our awareness to pivot to something beyond ourselves and others, to a significance of place, land, earth's sphere, and all other living matter. Ecofeminism

displaces the egocentrality of our work, the work that privileges all things human, many times at the expense of all things not human. As a sociopolitical movement, on one level it draws parallels between the oppression of nature and the oppression of women, and on another level (there are many, even though I am highlighting only the two extremes) it combines feminist politics with ecological awareness to redirect and transform the possibilities of a sustainable environment. In its more politically interesting discussions, it combines eco-anarchism and anarcha-feminist work to push the boundaries of radical or social democracy, where hierarchical power is seen as the root of many inequities and abuses of nature. As part of ecofeminism's objectives, sustainable communities are small groups where equilibrium of power, needs, and responsibilities is created through feminist politics. It is also transnational, delving into the politics of geography, culture, and ecology. Now that popular cultural structures have deemed the environment to be at risk (the Academy of Motion Picture Arts and Sciences award *An Inconvenient Truth* an Oscar, automobile companies manufacture hybrid cars, celebrities use their fame to bring awareness to the environmental crises, earth-friendly products pop up everywhere, "buy local" incentives are pushed throughout communities, and the list goes on), there is a growing urgency to be involved, to play one's part in saving the Earth. Ecofeminism indulges and challenges essentialist, popular, and critical perspectives in ecology, environmentalism, and globalization, offering richly engaging discussions about the application of a feminist politics in the ecosphere.

Virtual gender, otherwise known as cyberfeminism, perhaps originated with Donna Haraway's "A Cyborg Manifesto" in 1985. Chela Sandoval pushed it further in 1995 and discussed "cyborg" as a technique, a method of the oppressed to survive in a techno-human culture. She unfolds five different technologies people employ to survive:

sign reading, deconstruction, meta-ideologizing, democratics, and differential movement. At the cusp of a new century, the idea of virtual gender and cyberfeminism took a detour into constructed worlds in cyberspace from role-playing games, video games, chat rooms, instant messaging, text messaging, blogs, virtual reality, virtual spaces and identities, cybercrime, and many other sites and areas. Gender is constructed and transgressed. What sparked my own curiosity was the prevalence of men playing female characters and vice versa in online multiplayer games. This phenomenon I quickly learned is known as "gender swapping." Online characters enact virtual gender with a different degree of freedom through the fiction of online environments. Virtual gender/cyberfeminism lends a new understanding to postmodernism, post-structuralism, hyper-reality, and simulacra. The literature is grounded worldwide and in multiple disciplines, as one might suspect, such as computer science, technology and information systems, communication studies, digital media arts, women's and gender studies, psychology, and sociology. An intriguing aspect of virtual gender is the attention being paid to citizenship, democracy, and community development in the ethics of virtual spaces. It is a very porous membrane that separates online worlds from "real" worlds. Virtual gender, as a subfield of the previously mentioned disciplines, deals with gendered access to technology, consumption, pleasure and desire, sociopolitical and cultural concerns, designer responsibility, reflexivity and narrative, and shifting boundaries between "natural" and "virtual" realities/subjectivities (Green & Adam, 2001). With the proliferation of access to a multitude of media outlets—especially as handheld devices carry greater capacity and online connections are available via wireless networks—parallel issues can carry over to virtual spaces with less accountability. What twists and turns will feminist theories take through wireless paths?

teachers

Youth as Docents and Underground/ Multi-ground Sites of Resistance

In this section I do two things: I spend a significant amount of text space on youth as important docents[1] for the next steps in feminist theorizing and activism, and I focus on feminist collectives operating in various places in the United States and internationally. These are interesting examples of theory in action and sites for further research. The vibrancy of feminist theories in education will depend on the ways we continue to research, learn, and explore what else exists without forgetting what has been. It is at the intersection of history and the present that we can envision a more creative future. With that said, let's turn to youth.

Youth are often seen as the quintessential representation of the future, hope, and possibility—if they are not pathologized, criminalized, demonized, or medicated beforehand. Yet youth are rarely prepared or schooled to delve into discourses of both critique and hope. Youth usually search for meaning, regardless of whether they are instructed to, often without a productive outlet to really just be or explore who they are or want to be. So they must constantly struggle to guard themselves while trying to reach out for connections and acceptance. Youth solidify their identities by seeking cohesion, collectivity, and validation from peers and society at large, yet the educational system does little to nurture or help them question who they think they are.

In "Creativity, Art, and Aesthetics Unraveled through Post-formalism: An Exploration of Perception, Experience, and Pedagogy" (Villaverde 1999), I play with the concept of imagination as a great tool/space/sketchpad for working out one's ideas, emotions, visions, and possibilities without directly or immediately putting these into play with the outside world. The imagination can be a buffer, a moment of deep reflexivity and creativity where one can slow things down for deeper engagements. Thus I classify "imagination" as a fourth dimension (at the risk of sounding like science fiction), a space that can be included within the educational terrain through which to examine or test external knowledge with internal and familiar interpretations. Critical analysis is allowed a secret way in, without jeopardizing whatever image youth have constructed for themselves. Within this dimension or space, imagination may offer a new perspective, a way to let guards down safely, decentering previous knowledge and redefining what has been learned. The imagination preserves the private in a way that allows for the public (self) not to be threatened as easily, facilitating a freer acceptance of the unfamiliar, of difference.

Nisbet (1976) questions, What else is imagination but the moving around in the mind, restlessly, compulsively, so often randomly, of images with which to express and contain some aspect of perceived reality? It is this perceived reality and images we hold on to that construct our inner realities, helping define who we are (not), what roles we may undertake or aspire to. So what if, through feminist theories and activism experienced in many contexts (educational, social, recreational, online, etc.), we expand the resources for these images, realities, constructs of identity? What might youth do with access to greater agency earlier? What might the world be? If only we had the courage to imagine, to take the risks, feel the alienation, and to endure the sacrifice of seeing the world through critical lenses and carving divergent paths for social change.[2]

As a personal site for political work, the imagination cultivates the not-yet and reclaims democratic practices in education (or any pedagogical site) as it exercises the young's individual rights to freedom, social justice, equity, culture, gender representation, and sexual expression. The imagination grants validity to their voice, at least initially, as they safely contemplate alternatives and possibilities outside of anyone's criticism or intervention. Collectively, the cultivation of imagination, reflective thinking, and critical consciousness enables youth to discern and augment their sense of agency. They may approach

learning eager, motivated, or agitated. This agitation is an essential catalyst for political theorizing and action.[3] Acknowledging the force within imagination does not guarantee that it will be used in a socially progressive manner. Yet acknowledgment is the first of many steps for a socially conscious and responsible usage of the imagination{AQ: "usage" of what?}. Marcuse (1978) contends these are the inner resources of the human being: "passion, imagination, and conscience" (p. 5).

The imagination equally affords the space to contemplate another's reality, providing a (tentative, temporal) simulated experience of walking in someone else's shoes.[4] Carefully engaging (not appropriating) someone else's eyes without renouncing our own perspective creates a double (or triple, quadruple, and so on) consciousness,[5] a sense of understanding two or more worlds simultaneously, consequently expanding our own when we shed, SHED the other's shoes. We then can develop both an individual and a social or ethical conscience and solidify our passion and purpose. Hartman (1993) calls it "a sympathetic imagination: an identification with experiences or stories not our own" (p. 246), although empathy, instead of sympathy, may more aptly sidestep the possibility of being condescending or patronizing while allowing for the **unintelligibility** of the other. For youth, within the context of any learning site, this becomes a valuable tool in realizing they are not alone while crossing unthinkable borders and that people, places, things (life) are not entirely knowable. These guided experiences are strictly that: guided, initially, in order to attempt to maximize and structure the freedom within the possibilities of the imagination. This undoubtedly forces a significant degree of reform in feminist discourse and pedagogy.

Young people of all gender and ethnic, racial, and sexual identifications author the most contemporary trade discourses in feminist theorizing and activism.[6] Many of them use lived experience (even academic ones), pop culture, current policy and events, family, and community to write about how

Unintelligibility

the condition of not being able to be understood or made sense of; or being incomprehensible

and where feminism lives. These reclaim a social and pragmatic freedom to conceptualize, create, and discuss the not-yet or marginalized in unheard-of ways. In essence, these discourses expand the fixed conditions in which one creates and speaks about one's life, theorizing, or activism and others' works, and act to complicate/redefine the wealth of representations that shape both individual and collective identities. There are no apologies in how they represent the world. So it is no surprise that these works are also afflicted by stereotypes, binaries, or unquestioned truisms, but such moments can be utilized as springboards for poignant feminist critical inquiry, to know our own position better, driven to ask even more critical questions.

This reading for alterity should be happening in any pedagogical setting as a given, not as a novelty or trend. To underscore what I discussed in the visual studies section, the intensity and pervasiveness of our visual culture can be instrumental in instigating more direct, or raw, feminist discourses. Youth will undoubtedly continue to utilize visual and popular culture as the space for theorizing, learning, and intellectualizing about social, political, economic, and global issues. My argument here is that most current trade feminist discourses are already employing the imagination as I have described it above. These young "women" and "men" may not have framed their theorizing through the imagination, but the work exhibits the active use of the imagination as, if nothing else, a temporary site for organizing and understanding what they know and what they have experienced.

And what about feminist collectives, underground, and multi-ground sites for resistance? How do these fit in to the currency of our discourse? Feminist collectives are some of the most interesting grounds for activism, models of commitment, and diversity. I include them in this chapter on contemporary discourses to highlight where such **in situ** dialogue occurs, to shift our attention from institutions of learning to the theory created in other, equally dynamic sites for education.

In situ
in place, localized; a natural or original position

Mujeres Creando are an anarcha-feminist collective in Bolivia started in the 1990s by three women, Julieta Paredes, Maria Galindo, and Monica Mendoza. They use street theater, propaganda, and direct engagement, mainly through the creative arts, to speak against poverty, machismo, racism, anti-gay prejudice, and neoliberalism in the country. Ainger (2002) reports, "At the time, they explain, there was little talk of feminism—a militant, radical feminism, a feminism of the streets, of everyday life" (p. 107). Mujeres Creando publish a newspaper titled *Mujer Publica* and use graffiti as their main tool to communicate their critique of various political parties. The collective use the streets as their theater, canvas, and podium, as they believe the streets are of the people in Bolivia. They helped another collective called Deudora, a group of women protesting against the rising interest rates for small loans. The two groups collaborated over several months on mural after mural describing or protesting against the inequity; they threatened and organized against the Banking Supervisory agency. They finally organized a meeting with the agency to sign an agreement that served the interests of the organizers and suspended the accrued debt. On their website, http://www.mujerescreando.com, they explain who they are, what they do, and what they hope to accomplish. On the site (which is in Spanish) they describe their current activist work, ways to contact them, and how they continue to spread their message.

La Rivolta! are a feminist collective in Boston and Buenos Aires (although the branch in Boston is currently inactive); they aim to create spaces for social change and revolution. The collective in Buenos Aires demonstrate their concern by directly mobilizing against the abuse of power in families, schools, workplaces, and relationships. They carefully articulate the lived reality of power, where it is found, and through what it is exercised, and detail their multiple actions against oppression. In 1998 they bought a house and refurbished it, to open in 2004. Named Casita de Colores, the house is a social center for liberty where they organize lunches or

dinners; book, article, and pamphlet discussions; writing projects; a library; movie viewings; youth education; and any other social collaboration for political or cultural change. The collective offer workshops about a variety of social issues to further inform, educate, and learn together about not only individual responsibility but social accountability. One of the most amazing actions of the center is the provision of different services and cooperatives for anyone in need. They provide printing services, unemployment and employment services, and support groups. La Rivolta! appear to be extremely well organized and thriving for different communities.

MicroRevolt are a collective focusing on sweatshops, early industrial capitalism, and the feminization of labor. They are also concerned with global expansion and how consumerism and labor are used to spread injustice. They produce knitwear with logos from sweatshop offenders, have knitted a large Nike swoop blanket as a petition to demonstrate support for Nike garment workers, and protest against labor abuses worldwide. For the petition blanket, interested parties should knit a 4 × 4–inch square and mail it to MicroRevolt as their signature. They are also connected to many other organizations and nonprofits working toward the same goal. Gender is a central issue in labor disputes, grievances, and injustices. Their website is http://www.microrevolt.org.

Radical Knitting aims to "challenge the cultural and social norms demanded by a bourgeois-capitalist-racist-homophobic-cornflake-eating society" (http://www.ms.unimelb.edu.au/~paul/radical.html). They believe through knitting odd but wearable things in unexpected places that their presence disrupts the status quo. Their aim is to start many random political conversations with strangers. In their conversations they will discuss queer rights, democracy, war, anarchy, and so on. As the group or individuals sit and knit in different places, they make themselves accessible for dialogue, using the act of knitting as a catalyst.

Bunnies on Strike are a feminist collective in The Netherlands working for improved protection and

regulation in the sex industry. They were inspired by the Playboy Bunnies strike in 1975, when the women employed as Bunnies protested for the improvement of their work environment. On their website the first thing you find is the following quote:

> In essence, Feminism is about recognizing the oppression and inequality that exists within the world, and doing something about it. Feminism is not meant to be a movement that excludes men or makes women the superior sex. It is about creating a harmonious, respectful society that is willing to share its resources, rights, and powers with people of both sexes and all colors. (http://www.bunniesonstrike.cjb.net)

Initially, Bunnies on Strike started as a zine; now they have a website, spoken word, radical cheerleading, music festivals, and many other projects in progress. Their zines and radical cheers are available on the website. Critical of practically everything, they regard shopping as a political act, so they encourage people to create their personalized Bunnies on Strike merchandise (how-to directions are provided). One T-shirt they display states "Make your tshirt = textbook!" (text tees are very popular in the United States, but we usually do not discuss them as educational activism). To them, cheerleading is "a ridiculous activity" and they have decided to radicalize and use it almost as performance art at concerts, demonstrations, festivals, and on any street. All of their cheers are political, and anyone is invited to join, provided they practice with the group.

Another cheerleading group is NYC Radical Cheerleaders, a "collectively run radical cheerleading squad comprised of queer, straight and transgendered women and men, youth and adults living in the boroughs of New York City" (http://www.nycradicalcheerleaders.org). Their cheers are documented from 1999 on, and they have made an award-wining documentary of their story. Their current squad is active in a variety of social issues; among their priorities are education, sexism and

street harassment, positive body image and sex-positive education, and racism (their website has the full list). They see radical cheerleading as having been a global movement since 1997, started by two sisters in Florida. Most squads are feminist, anarchist, and anti-capitalist, yet each collective organizes its own politics. They believe in making participation in dissent fun and engaging others to get more people involved.

The last two groups I discuss are perhaps slightly more academic or theoretical but similarly dynamic. NextGENDERation "is a transnational European network of students, researchers and activists with an interest in feminist theory and politics, and their intersections with anti-racist, migrant, lesbian, queer and anti-capitalist struggles" (http://www.nextgenderation.net). They have various working groups around the world and email is the unifying entity whereby new groups are formed and information about what is happening is dispersed. Truly working as a network, these multiple collectives actively theorize many topics pertaining to feminist politics and gender studies. Each collective decides what source of activism is germane to its priorities and geography.

A similar collective is subRosa, "a reproducible cyberfeminist cell of cultural researchers committed to combining art, activism, and politics to explore and critique the effects of the intersections of the new information and biotechnologies on women's bodies, lives, and work" (http://www.cyberfeminism.net/index.html). They produce artworks and media interventions as their form of activist campaigns and projects. On their website they list their publications, artworks, and a DVD dating back almost a decade. Their interests in gender, health, and globalization produce thought-provoking public engagements and seek new "affirmative alliances and coalitions." Their site chronicles various public works and events and provides more information about the intersection of their political commitments.

All of the feminist collectives discussed here engage in a wide range of topics and activism. Even

though this is only a small sample of all the work that exists, it illustrates the concerted efforts to disrupt the public sphere informed by feminist theory and politics. Simply because certain works may not be highly visible does not mean these are not there and in full operation. I highlight these points to demonstrate the range of issues and ways the public is engaged only to push for more possibilities for activism and cultural, social, and political work.

Parting Thoughts on Contemporary Discourses

In this chapter, perhaps more so than in any other, I was trapped by language. First, "contemporary": the minute I write or designate something "contemporary," whether it is a discourse, field of study, or collective, it ceases to be so. The temporality of its currency is undeniable; regardless, I need some way to mark the importance of its relative newness while understanding the intersectionality of discourses that have existed for quite some time. The artificial demarcations between discourses I find problematic; where something ends, starts, or differs is largely arbitrary, *especially* through postmodern, post-structural, feminist lenses. It was not easy to give just enough information to provide an entry into these discourses and ideas and not become encyclopedic or monolithic. Take these as they are: prompts for dialogue that need to be explored, continued, and challenged. I chose gender studies, masculinity studies, queer studies, transnational studies, and visual studies for what they offer feminist work and the connections we can establish in pedagogical sites for cutting-edge possibilities. Perhaps I have an insatiable desire for ever-expanding ways of looking and learning and I am projecting or, worse, universalizing this personal indulgence, or I am helping to legitimize the potential for hybridity, amalgams, or fusions, for voices that do not quite fit here or there, but somewhere in between. I hope it comes across as the latter. The focus on youth is out of a commitment to see younger people become more

confident about themselves and their place in the world, to see them develop new connections and perspectives on the world we inhabit, and to chart fresh paths for intervening in social injustices, as well as to keep people connected to learning despite schooling and beyond educational institutions. In short, I would like to broaden positive youth development. Finally, the limited sample of feminist collectives offers an entry into the incredibly hard work of living one's politics in socially productive ways.

GLOSSARY

Countercultural narratives—perspectives resisting or subverting normative culture, society, or the status quo

Disidentification—the questioning of and distancing from, in order to transform, traditional identification practices and culture

In situ—in place, localized; a natural or original position

Interdisciplinarity—the involvement of two or more disciplines; an integration of concepts, ideas, and practices across disciplines for more holistic studies

Transgressive—exceeding, advancing, or crossing a boundary or border of social expectation or acceptability

Unintelligibility—the condition of not being able to be understood or made sense of; or being incomprehensible

CHAPTER FOUR

Feminist Research Analysis

How we inquire about the world and the people around us matters. How we study lived experience and theoretical constructions matters to how we act in the world, which notions we perpetuate, and which ones we restructure. Feminist theories inform, guide, and challenge the ways we explore and investigate local and global issues, yet we spend insufficient time critically analyzing how we engage the world politically. I feel both a pedagogical and theoretical need to step back and delve further into the systems of thinking that frame our consciousness and actions. The goal of this chapter is to focus on the analysis of epistemology and ideology, subjectivity and positionality, and the politics of recognition and action in and through feminist research.

One might ask, Why engage in the analysis of research rather than in the practice of doing feminist research? I find that many times we jump into doing for the sake of doing: anxious to be involved in action, we disregard the benefits of active thinking and analysis, particularly its use in guiding our

actions and advocacy. Research is but one conduit of activism, but if we just *do* without carefully, methodically *doing* we run the risk of perpetuating the very practices and ideas we intend to debunk and rework. Critical analysis is also mainly seen as a solitary endeavor, something that is assumed to be done in a vacuum, disconnected from engagement, from the collective, yet one of the ways many of us learn is through dialogue, and feminist research analysis is crystallized in egalitarian conversation. We neglect and underestimate the power of conversation in scholarly work and evaluation. Feminist research analysis is but one way to recapture the benefits of rigorous theorizing in reading, study, and dialogue.

In addition, the examination of feminist approaches to philosophical and practical inquiries prepares us to read research critically and to understand the place of gender in lived experiences and institutional spaces. Most important, this chapter dwells on the rules and ideas that govern inquiry decisions and methods. These conventions are shaped by ideologies and theories that construct what questions to ask, what problems to detect, and what analysis to produce. Too often research paradigms are glossed over, pushed behind the scenes, and obscured. Among my main goals is not only to expose the strings that mobilize the marionette, so to speak, but to comprehend the nature of knowledge production and critical inquiry. To extend the metaphor, my goal is also for readers to develop ways of seeing and manipulating the strings that control movement and direction as it is applied to feminism. If we think of each string as representations of theories, ideologies, epistemologies, intentions, visions, convictions, or any other particular that is enacted, we begin to see agency behind these movements. This agency, intertwined with subjectivity and **reflexivity**, provides an ample stage for critical inquiry.

I also refrain from anointing (as if I could) particular methods as feminist. To do so would be to lock in definitions and categorizations of feminism

Reflexivity

a critical awareness of the researcher's engagement or participation in the inquiry process and of her or his epistemological choices in the research design, implementation, and articulation that I have purposely left open throughout the book for the reader to determine. According to Brayton (1997), "it has become apparent that what makes feminist research uniquely feminist are the motives, concerns and knowledge brought to the research process," not one method or methodology. This does not mean that feminist research methods are difficult to conceptualize, define, or execute; on the contrary, the literature is expansive on various methods and studies. What I offer is slightly off of certainty (instead of center), as I believe authors such as Shulamit Reinharz, Nancy Naples, Gloria Anzaldúa, Emma Pérez, Sandra Harding, Michelle Fine, Patti Lather, Daphne Patai, Sharlene Nagy Hesse-Biber, Bronwyn Davies, Laurel Richardson, Lubna Nazir Chaudhry, Donna E. Alvermann, Wanda Pillow, Elizabeth A. St. Pierre, Patricia Leavy, Connie Miller, Corinna Treitel, Joey Sprague, Deborah Britzman, Michelle Yaiser, Marjorie DeVault, Leslie Bloom, and countless others provide excellent research texts illustrating both theoretical considerations and concrete examples. Their work has been instrumental for me, and I invite readers to study their feminist insights and maps for inquiry carefully. This chapter builds on their work by focusing on the complexity of research decisions and actions through the idea of the *trickster*.

The trickster often stands, in fact revels, in the between spaces of reality, negotiation, intention, desire, and the unknown. There are many definitions of tricksters from archetypes to deviants; however, one is most useful here: the trickster as "antagonistic agent of uncertainty" (Kazmierczak, 2001, p. 143). Thus I propose the researcher embody the antagonistic agent of uncertainty as it more appropriately captures the precipice the researcher is constantly on or should occupy. If the researcher is curious enough to study a particular phenomenon before embarking on designing more ways to learn about it, she or he must balance what is known and not known, not only though the development stage of research but throughout the research, and through the writing of it as well. The researcher needs to

know enough, yet not be locked in, and must be willing to unlearn for the sake of what is yet to be learned and done. The feminist trickster wishes to induce cognitive dissonance, dislodging our attachment to the way things are, to the status quo. She or he unlocks hybridity, potential, and creativity through extensive critique and analysis. The tools of the trickster researcher develop from the investigation and interrogation of epistemology and ideology, subjectivity and positionality, the politics of recognition, and action. Trickster researchers search for ways to understand what is known, what is privileged and marginalized, who they are as a result, what responsibility they have in instigating and producing change, and how they may provoke others to get involved. Keeping the trickster in mind, next we move to understanding the paradigms that underwrite the rules and regulations of research and inquiry.

Before delving into the key components (epistemology and ideology, subjectivity and positionality, the politics of recognition, and action) of feminist research analysis, it seems instructive to explain paradigmatic controversies and the hegemonies these tend to produce (Lincoln & Guba, 2000). Traditional paradigms such as positivism and postpositivism prescribe distinct relationships between subject and object, as well as methods of inquiry. Traditional paradigms separate logic and emotion and isolate social factors from the object of study. Validity and reliability factors are pivotal elements that render a study valuable or not, measuring its significance in the quest for certainty and truth. Survey questions must go through layers of screening for accuracy and objectivity.

Postmodern paradigms such as critical theory, constructivism, and participatory structures challenge the relationship between knower and known, in addition to what can be known and how. Postmodern paradigms highlight multiple subjectivities, search for various truths, and expose where power resides. They expose the embeddedness of **logocentrism** and **androcentrism** in traditional

Logocentrism

a method of analysis that privileges reason, logic, and truth as a way to understand reality

Androcentrism

an analytic concept placing masculine perspectives as the foundation for societal beliefs and practices; these perspectives are universalized as normative for any member of society inquiry processes while stressing the importance of reflecting on one's subjectivity and agency. These paradigms prescribe specific values in the construction, experience, and discussion of research. Knowledge may be exposed or discarded depending on the lens through which it is found. Certain methods tend to be associated with either positivism or constructivism; lines are demarcated between quantitative and qualitative methods, or superficially blurred in integrated methods. The instructiveness of analyzing these paradigms, methodologies, and methods lies in the possibility of delinking method or technique from large paradigms and ultimately having greater access to disrupt the public and private status quo through the use of research. In other words, research becomes a strategic tool for activism and intervening in public and private inequity; thus the trickster is provoked in the context of these choices.

Epistemology and Ideology

Epistemology is the study of knowledge, its nature, origin, limits, and methods. It outlines certain conjectures about knowledge: what can be known, and through what methods it can be known. Ideology is a system of ideas, values, politics, or beliefs that shapes or explains a particular social order and informs ways of being for both individuals and groups. It characterizes views about the world and actions within it. Both epistemologies and ideologies shape the way research is designed, implemented, and articulated. In the search for objectivity and certainty, epistemologies are cleverly masked, as well as coded. Epistemologies or ideologies are also used to collude in the quest for objectivity. These practices communicate unfortunate implications about readers or knowers, essentially that readers cannot consider or truly understand the full spectrum of information available to them through deconstructing terminology and epistemologies. Clearly understanding both epistemologies and ideologies is crucial to an informed research practice. Being able

Genealogy
a tracing of ancestry and historicizing of the subject through the construction of knowledges, discourses, and social practices

to trace or map a **genealogy** of thought in any particular research study arms the researcher or student with critical information about the nature, purpose, and intent of the study. This information can be used as a tool to decode the limitations and implications of the study. Attention to the epistemologies and ideologies of the study or researcher can be improved through the information exposed.

The argument here is to tease out the epistemological and ideological background of any study to be prepared to comprehend, design, and implement research more accurately. There should be no doubt that we are influenced by and situated in epistemological and ideological stances, since from these we act on all sorts of theoretical assumptions. Too often these stances and assumptions are naturalized or presumed missing. Both of these dispositions incur a certain blindness counterproductive to critical consciousness or engaged action.

The problem arises when one's blindness or conditional awareness damages or impedes another human being, when one's privilege restricts someone else's. These are just some of the consequences. Knowing does not automatically guarantee insight or action, much less political consciousness, yet when it comes to research, one is setting oneself up directly to affect others; therefore, the luxuries (if some see it that way) of not knowing or caring are significantly decreased. Given the intention of research to study, learn, and engage the world, researchers must tread lightly before becoming involved in research. Researchers can slip into the trickster mode to inhabit these in-between spaces temporally but significantly, in turn to proceed or emerge politicized. With a distinct sense of urgency, the researcher delves into epistemological and ideological analyses to maximize the potential for social or political impact or action, if indeed feminist research is to create cultural change. The researcher's responsibility is amplified greatly, and thus one needs to engage in self-critical reflection before beginning one's research.

Subjectivity and Positionality

One significant contribution of feminist research is the careful attention it has paid to the researcher's subjectivity and positionality. I recognize subjectivity as the umbrella term inclusive of notions of positionality. I delineate them separately below to define each more clearly and then discuss subjectivity as an encompassing term. The researcher's subjectivity is constructed through reflexive engagement with, and critical analysis of, the self through multifaceted theorizing of ideologies, lived experience, and proleptic (not-yet) visions. This reflexivity often creates interesting paradoxes as the researcher wrestles with being the authority (outsider guiding inquiry) and the researched (insider identifying with what or who is studied). The trickster turns the trick and scrutinizes the self, and the mirror reflects the ambiguities of constructed realities and the transparent responsibility of one's alleged enlightenment.

Positionality is the result of how one is situated through the intersection of power and the politics of gender, race, class, sexuality, ethnicity, culture, language, and many other social registers that shape who we are. It is in this intersection that the trickster resides for a wider range of vision, perception, and clarity. Instead of the panopticon from above, it is 360-degree wideawakedness[1] from within. Traditional research paradigms obscure the researcher in hopes of preserving objectivity, certainty, and validity. The above introspections are regarded as liabilities not assets in complicating the sanctity of the research process. As feminist theories intersect various methodologies, how the researcher is situated (and her/his awareness of this) in both identity politics and discourse has a tremendous effect on the nature and outcome of research. Articulating subjectivity and further understanding positionality allow the reader to make fundamental connections between the intentionality, subjectivity or objectivity, and design of research. These undoubtedly frame how the research is lived and experienced.

Subjectivity is not without limitations. In recognizing where you are situated, you immediately identify where you are not; therefore, one's subjectivity is a shifting entity, evolving with every lived and learned experience. Regardless of its evolution or shifts, researchers must grapple with the intricacies of exploring, analyzing, and articulating their subjectivity. This allows for discernment in the quality of experience and consequent constructed knowledge.

Embodying the trickster here is incredibly useful, as the trickster is a boundary or border crosser recognizing limits, articulating margins, speaking the unsaid, and carving out new territories, many times through a certain levity, reminding us that margins and centers can be arbitrary.[2] Spinks (2001) continues, "[The trickster's] very being lies in paradox, contradiction, and the weaving of cultural unsaids with the unwavering of cultural pronouncements" (p. 14). The trickster lays out a process for the discussion of subjectivity, the ins and outs of who we are as it relates to present inquiries, the detours theories take through experience, the impression these make on what actions we take and what we stand for or against. The trickster becomes a conduit for knowledge delegitimized, perspectives and narratives not heard, legends to topographies of new maps, and thus, most important, a means for decentering fossilized practices. The next section takes up where the investigation of epistemologies, ideologies, and subjectivity provides the foundation for recognizing difference as a catalyst for social change and justice.

Politics of Recognition

What is the importance of deconstructing research and inquiry through the above subcategories or of using the trickster as an embodied means in this process? Why is doing so enacting particular feminist consciousnesses (*mestiza* and differential), and why should this be a preferred mode of action? These are common questions among students of feminist research. Understanding the ways in which research paradigms and epistemologies are organized, and how one's positionality is situated as a result, arms the researcher with a wealth of information useful in advocating or critically analyzing the production of knowledge and politics of inequity. Engaging in research through feminist theory allows the inquirer to use politicized knowledge to transform social conditions and mindsets and to propose possibilities in public institutions that affect people's everyday lives. This is not to suggest that any of this is a guaranteed outcome; on the contrary, there is never any guarantee of political insight. Yet, through holding oneself accountable by keeping to the above factors, there is an increased potential for deeper engaged activist uses of research insights.

There are two concepts I want to stress as an outcome of feminist research, a politics of recognition and action (the latter is discussed in the last section of the chapter). One critical role of feminist research is to augment the ways we recognize the self and others, to understand the politics of dismissal and marginalization and what actions we take as a result. Research can have a significant impact on the ways in which people, experiences, and conditions are acknowledged. What is studied carries more political weight than one might think. Charles Taylor introduced the politics of recognition into multicultural discourses prevalent in the early 1990s, proposing that the central issue for minorities was the lack of political recognition within mainstream society. Taylor was criticized for his liberal understanding of difference and the limited scope of recognition. Andersson (2000) countered with a situated politics of recognition built around a process and context-oriented social epistemology where recognition is not solely based on potentially stereotypic ethnic categories. Although I lean toward Andersson's conceptualization, I would like to trouble it further by bringing our awareness to the struggle of being recognized and the ensuing encapsulation of that recognition.

A central concern of feminist research (and feminism in general) is to make androcentrism, logocentrism, and patriarchy explicit, to expose the ways these create and shape the world around us and how these operations of power disenfranchise and oppress "women," "men," and those who identify as neither. As a result of such a mission, there is a continued struggle to recognize the unrecognized, yet through this process gender and experiences are made static, which brings us back to Taylor. What I argue for is, yes, a recognition of underrepresentation, as well as the structures that produce these two-dimensional identities, but also an acknowledgment of the incongruencies of identity, the shifting, conflicting, contradictory roles calling into question binaries and boundaries of gender, sexuality, and other social constructs of self and others. These contradictions, or seemingly opposing forces, are not seen as needing to be resolved or unified; they are accepted as is, as part of the crux of living. There is no ill angst, only productive angst (like productive alienation[3]) that instigates clearer insight into how we understand the use of theory, praxis, and research in everyday life and, ideally, policy.

The trickster again is helpful here as she or he often embodies polar opposites, contrasting elements that are explicit in society yet incomplete because they are perpetually caught in some seesaw effect, ricocheting off each other without ever being altered by the impact or friction. Instead of providing a distant comfortable space to unleash these binaries, the trickster can force us to increase what we recognize and why. Through this figure we can take greater ownership of walking the mindfields of self, experience, knowledge, and other. Anzaldúa (2002) asks, "What if freedom from categories occurs by widening the psyche/body's borders, widening the consciousness that senses self (the body is the basis for the conscious sense of self, the representation of self in the mind)?" (p. 555). What we recognize in others, psychodynamically speaking, often mirrors fears, desires, or fragments in ourselves. So

in pushing the politics of recognition to encompass more than predetermined identity categories, we employ what we learned from the above investigations into our epistemologies, ideologies, and subjectivity to expand what we are capable of understanding in others. This deeper recognition in both self and others establishes the foundation for building coalitions of solidarity.

I also want to say a few words about methodologies and methods (a theory of how research is done or should proceed, or guidelines for carrying out a particular inquiry project; a technique or a way of proceeding—respectively, Harding, 1987, and Jamieson, 2007[4] as strategies for this recognition. I have purposely stayed away from charting different feminist methods since my argument is that any method can be feminist or utilized for feminist purposes. It depends on the above discussions. Yet looking at research in this way places the onus on the researcher to articulate his or her intent, purpose, means, and ends carefully, so that the reader or participant of the research can assess holistically whether it was a feminist endeavor and be informed or educated on what that is. Some of the authors listed earlier in this chapter question the parameters they employ to define their research as feminist (others see it as a given). This is the purpose of first delving into the epistemologies and ideologies that inform one's project and situatedness before designing and conducting any research. The ways we use a renewed politics of recognition can dramatically increase the substance in the process of inquiry; nuances and uncertainties can be profoundly studied, and the consequences of research can provoke greater flexibility in living.

Laurel Richardson's concept of crystallization is instructive here as well. She offers this as a substitute for triangulation, a common strategy for the combination of methodologies, points of view, or data. Richardson (2000) contends, "We recognize that there are far more than three sides by which to approach the world . . . the central imaginary for validity for postmodernist texts is not the triangle .

. . [it is] the crystal, which combines symmetry and substance with an infinite variety of shapes, substances, transmutations, multidimensionalities, and angles of approach"—and of living, I would add (p. 13). Through this crystallization, she affirms, we will know more and be dislodged from what we think we know. Thus the power of this nonsynchronicity[5] generates paths for critical consciousness and political action. In 1993, Anna Deavere Smith, a talented political artist, wrote and performed in *Fires in the Mirror: Crown Heights, Brooklyn, and Other Identities,* a play about black, Jewish, and white racial tensions and riots, after the avoidable deaths of a black boy and a young Jewish man in 1991. In this performance she keenly advises knowing as an antidote to perpetuating hatred, and vocabulary begetting or leading to general awareness. Through crystallizing the elements of feminist research analysis we can contribute to this antidote as we carve new spaces for praxis.

Action

There is a call to action brewing in research that is either designated as feminist or self-identified as such. Similar to the need to translate theory into action for critical theorists, Lincoln and Guba (2000) argue there are "degrees of social action, from overturning of specific unjust practices to radical transformation of entire societies. The call to action—whether in terms of internal transformation, such as ridding oneself of false consciousness, or of external social transformation" (p. 174). The need to act feels like a freight train getting closer and closer as the horn gets louder and louder; hence, even with the incredible progress made on issues of gender and sexuality, more tactical work must occur. I use the word "must" with extreme intent in troubling historical times, with the ever-looming complete reversal of *Roe v. Wade,* continued pay inequity (still 77 cents to the dollar), granting of same-sex marriages and revocation of those same rights, compromises to family leave acts, reproductive rights restrictions, violence against women and sexual minorities rising (worldwide), and, frankly, too many other daily injustices. The transnational landscape is worse; gendered rights are intermittent if they exist at all. Unless research is understood as a necessary phase of activism, any sociopolitical-cultural impact continues to accrue only in small increments despite the monumental significance of some of these acts. If I sound cataclysmic, the intention is to alert the student of research and the current researcher to comprehend the small window of possibility that exists in the choices made and through the reflexivity engaged. Feminist research analysis builds on the works of many excellent scholars and demands constant becomings, like **rhizoanalysis,** where the researcher is in a position to construct new knowledge, not perpetuate existing limitations, and interrogates the purpose, connectivity (heterogeneous and multiple), consequence, hierarchy, order, historicity, and multiple readings of any knowledge produced. Rhizoanalysis focuses on bringing forth what is there and what is not yet there, similar to the tactics of the trickster, teetering on the edge of representation and construction.

The trickster thrives in the interspace of razor-sharp analysis and visionary commentary, provoking action or reaction or any sort of movement. Tricksters understand their presence (subjectivity), where they are coming from (epistemology), what lens they operate through (ideology), and how they play with mirrors, reflections or visibility, and invisibility (politics of recognition) so that ruptures, deterritorializations, and reterritorializations[6] occur (actions). In these actions, tricksters work within and without; it is this interplay that gives them crystal clarity into possible breaks for change.

Another element of action that I would like to bring back to your attention is writing. I briefly mentioned it at the start of this chapter. If we see the benefit of spending the time necessary to analyze research in the way explained in this chapter, just as much attention should be spent on writing or documenting the process, analysis, and outcomes

---

Rhizoanalysis

a method of analysis mapping or connecting otherwise disparate entities or concepts; these connections allow for multiple points of entry to the discourse or inquiry, with new possibilities for knowledge production

of inquiries. Writing can provide many moments of displacement in one's thinking, in what was once understood. To allow this shift to take place sets the stage for a different type of future reading and writing. Border theory and writing can be exercised at this juncture for new considerations in the writing process. Hicks (1991) makes this clear by suggesting that writing is always a rereading, and a reading always a rewriting, a subversive act, a writing that disrupts the one-way flow of information. She expands in saying border writing is a process of negotiation between the referential codes of the author and reader and the logic or narrative strategies of texts in order to recognize the non-identities rendered unimportant by these codes.[7] Equal care in the articulation of research is critical to highlight its multidimensionality and possibilities. A note of caution should be sounded about the writing phase, however: remain mindful of generalizations from research insights or findings. It may be too easy to fall into a corrective mode toward status quo or mainstream practices of research. To assume one method (technique) is right or better than another replicates power in the same ways we have experienced it thus far, only inverting the hierarchy; for that reason, reflexivity is a fundamental pre-emptive strategy necessary for new types of border writing. Mohanty (2003) adds that writing and memory are critically significant in the creation of oppositional agency.

The activism/action phase materializes with the understanding of the power of the word and the ways this opens the reading of the world. To take what I write at face value does you and me a disservice. This text, any text, is an interactive plane through which many dimensions (interpretations) traverse and exist. These dimensions are the context where epistemology, ideology, and subjectivity intersect to provide multiple perspectives or reads and consequent calls to action. Key questions to ask are "What is the purpose of the text?" and "What purposes do these ideas provide for one's agency in the world?" Remember, knowledge does not lead directly to action; however, the decentering of assumed givens is a step in unexplored directions, the start of new movements. The leaps to action are many times difficult. These are replete with hesitation and uneasiness, whether it is the initial failure to return the gaze or felt marginalization or lack of confidence in questioning reality. Whatever may be the cause of paralysis, no action is still an action; therefore the moment of trepidation need not be ignored, but can be investigated and meta-analyzed for a wealth of feminist inquiries. These moments continuously permute in space and time continuums for infinite risks and prospects to exemplify the potential in human incompleteness.

The critical preludes to research practice are key to the success and enjoyment of the research process, yet it is equally necessary to add a pedagogical component to one's work. Unless the trickster is also a learner, she or he will not be able to embody the above spaces of uncertainty and transformation. How else do we learn if not through exposure, discussion, simulation, or experience? As part of the urgency to act, pedagogical action is just as relevant in the next turn for feminist theories. What we do in academic programs can infiltrate a proliferation of roles in society. Feminist programs of study are mostly interdisciplinary sites and therefore hold an audience of willing and unwilling participants. These are the spaces to engage the public and unleash the tricksters.

GLOSSARY

Androcentrism—an analytic concept placing masculine perspectives as the foundation for societal beliefs and practices; these perspectives are universalized as normative for any member of society

Genealogy—a tracing of ancestry and historicizing of the subject through the construction of knowledges, discourses, and social practices

Logocentrism—a method of analysis that privileges reason, logic, and truth as a way to understand reality

Reflexivity—a critical awareness of the researcher's engagement or participation in the inquiry process and of her or his epistemological choices in the research design, implementation, and articulation

Rhizoanalysis—a method of analysis mapping or connecting otherwise disparate entities or concepts; these connections allow for multiple points of entry to the discourse or inquiry, with new possibilities for knowledge production

CHAPTER FIVE

Feminist Pedagogy and Activism

What is feminist pedagogy, what does it do, and what can it do? Does it differ from critical pedagogy or from "good teaching," and, if so, how? What is the connection between feminist pedagogy and activism? Where does the impetus to collapse the alleged divide between theory and practice come from? What is necessary for intellectual freedom and how is the classroom a space for such discovery and action? These queries are common in both undergraduate and graduate classrooms as students grapple with new methods of knowledge production. In this chapter I address some misconceptions about the feminist classroom and some of its tenets, and I problematize the concepts of voice, authority, and rigor. First, I interrogate the weight we place on pedagogy, on the classroom space and dynamics, and on us as feminist educators.

Both educators and students come to the classroom with defenses, anxieties, hopes, passions, and numerous expectations about the quality of learning experiences. So much is riding on the chemistry

among the classroom participants and the interest and accessibility of the course content. Many times it is hit and miss, especially in professed feminist classrooms, where the need or expectation to connect and transform is, I believe, higher than in non-feminist spaces. As we delve into understanding feminist pedagogy, a clear awareness of these issues is crucial in the design and navigation of feminist learning experiences. Said imposition also increases an educator's responsibility for the success or failure of feminist pedagogies, or at least so we think. Realistically, when one's politics guide the ethics of any course, more will be at stake in the pedagogical process. This is where feminist pedagogy, critical pedagogy, and "good" teaching leak into one another. I suggest these are not separate types of pedagogies; theoretically they work from similar premises that pedagogy is an emancipatory process; it is about identity formation and the development of critical consciousness and political awareness. Central expectations are the development of critique and social change through an analysis of power and language. Identity is at the crux of these pedagogies, where race, gender, ethnicity, class, culture, sexuality, language, and other social categories detour theory and praxis for poignant meaning-making experiences. Depending on whether the emphasis of pedagogy is on gender or critical theory, the curricular goals may vary or shift, yet the overarching commonalities are change and awareness. Before delving further into the crossroads of pedagogy and action, let's take a few steps back to define core conceptualizations of feminist pedagogy and some of its tenets.

Feminist Pedagogy

I remain somewhat suspect of the term "feminist pedagogy," as it seems to drape a rather large blanket over certain pedagogical and philosophical practices. At times it creates many predicaments; sometimes it is not feminist enough for students, and other times it is disempowering for educators.

These intricate spaces in pedagogy are the consequence of varied philosophies of pedagogy and feminism. A common mistake is the belief that one or another type of pedagogy will be the sacred space many continuously desire. Yet the nature of engaged pedagogy, despite theoretical underpinnings, is an intellectual and physical jarring, a process of dislodging what was previously understood and envisioned. The assumed split or separation between theory and practice is a misconception; deep intellectual work should produce altered, or at least more informed, private and public acts. My own assumptions about pedagogy are grounded in seeing education as a vehicle for social change and transformation, an evolution of ideas and praxis. This is not to presume educational institutions generally work to this end; nonetheless feminist and critical pedagogies operate under the possibility and desire for making changes from within and without.

There is a wealth of literature on feminist pedagogy emphasizing the need for student voice, community, collaboration, democracy, empowerment, action, struggle, consciousness raising, and critique. These are just some of the tenets that are said to mark feminist pedagogy as such. At the heart of the learning experience are the fundamentals of political education: becoming aware of the issues at stake, developing a perspective, problem solving, and engaging in change, thus actively participating in both private and public spheres. Well-known scholars in feminist pedagogy such as bell hooks, Bernice Malka Fisher, Amie Macdonald, Susan Sanchez-Casal, Adriana Hernandez, Sofia Villenas, Barbara Omolade, Jennifer Gore, Frances Maher, Mary Kay Thompson Tetreault, Kathleen Weiler, and Patti Lather agree on the centrality of political knowledge production, a literacy of power and agency, and the social construction and (in)stability of identity. Fisher (2001) summarizes feminist pedagogy as "teaching that engages students in political discussion of gender injustice":

- This discussion is a collective, collaborative, and ongoing process that pays special attention to women's experiences, feelings, ideas, and actions.
- It seeks to understand and challenge oppressive power relations.
- It supports and generates women's political agency by addressing women's "personal" concerns and taking them seriously.
- It questions the meaning for differently situated women of oppression and liberation.
- It proceeds nonjudgmentally but cultivates the political judgment needed to act in response to gender and interwoven forms of injustice. (p. 44)[1]

Dialogue, reflection, and problem solving are common strategies in feminist classrooms as students are expected to understand theory through their diverse lived experiences. The danger of open dialogue as a strategy is over-reliance on the confessional moment (which may be couched in anti-intellectualism or essentialism of one voice as representative of all others in that specific identity location) and the slippage into narrative without critical reflexivity. The benefit is that many stories come into conversation with each other that highlight the rich nuances of power and politics in daily occurrences; a drawback is that these stories may be authenticated as frozen representations of difference. Just as speaking is encouraged, so should silence be, as it can be as edifying in terms of genuinely understanding both self and other. Since voice, participation, and community are so vital in feminist classrooms, careful attention needs to be given to their interaction in a closed shared space. Voice is not merely having the ability to speak, although sometimes this is a first step. Claiming or owning one's voice is the result of a process through which ideas, emotions, and experiences are critically analyzed and made public, not for the sake of disclosure in and of itself but for the furthering of collective knowledge production. The strategic use of one's political or public voice is about risking the self, and to some extent othering the self, as one thinks and speaks (or chooses not to think and speak) through multiple spaces. What happens in and through these verbal or bodily performances and utterances can easily shift power, so that a carefully choreographed democratic educational space swings off balance. The pedagogical space is a contested terrain, or at least it should be as learners in all roles come together to produce more insight and possibility in the continued support for diverse identities and experiences. The art of feminist pedagogy rests on the ability of both students and teacher to excavate the recurrent patterns of inequity and oppression, as well as the acts of transformation and activism.

Many feminist classrooms are built on the belief that education should be democratic and power-negotiated. When power is shared in the feminist classroom, sometimes in the hope of countering traditional patriarchal hierarchies, any evidence of power or authority is downplayed, creating new problems and a misunderstanding of the use of authority. Explicit power is replaced by giving up assumed power—"assumed" because it is not a given despite one's role as educator. This is a common reaction, an attempt to resolve previously experienced power imbalances or abuses; nevertheless, this only obscures where power resides and how it is wielded.

The existence of power is not the issue (we understand it is everywhere and operating in multiple directions); rather, how power is exercised and experienced is central to feminist pedagogy and discourse. Many feminist educators feel trapped by limitations of perceived shared power when the responsibility of the course's success rests largely on them. At the end of the semester, many still see classroom operations under the purview of professors as readings, assignments, and evaluations need to be given out and completed. The attempts at creating a democratic educational experience often can backfire, and educators are left open to ideological and pragmatic critique. Non-feminist classrooms

are in this sense protected by the absence of student participation, interrogation, or investment. Traditional educational conventions insist that power resides with the educator, yet the lived experiences of many faculty of color, women, and men who engage in feminist praxis relate counter-stories where their authority is devalued or their credibility is questioned openly. Education is neither neutral nor objective, and a feminist pedagogy catapults such critique to the forefront of the learning experience. Centralizing these issues in the curriculum, as well as negotiating issues of power and intellectual rigor, is a crucial experience in the feminist classroom; I am not arguing against it. I do want to underscore, however, how difficult it is to live and teach one's politics; as a result, in order to have meaningful or transformative learning experiences through feminist theory, we must be incredibly prepared and confident in understanding the urgency of, and sacrifices required for, such work.

Negotiating authority is equally tricky as educators try to balance sharing knowledge with student knowledge production. Too often feminist educators opt for their own silence in hopes of keeping to an interpretation of their chosen theoretical premise in classroom pedagogy. Both democratic intentions and authority are affected by a lack of clarity of how these are lived in pedagogical space. Negotiating the give and take of authority and establishing mutual respect, while pushing students to question existing knowledge and assumptions, is an ongoing, trying process. Educators have to know themselves well enough and be extremely confident in their intellect not to feel threatened by students' unpredictable learning paths. It is this comfort that will engender the excitement and possibility to be experienced in the classroom. Intellectual confidence and openness should not be confused with arrogance and inaccessibility. On the contrary, such confidence leads to **intellectual flexibility.** This is a term I often use in classes where I want students to extend what they know and how they know it, where I want them to entertain multiple/plural ways of under-

Intellectual flexibility
the ability to contend with various, sometimes opposing, ideas simultaneously for the sake of increasing agency and critical analysis

standing, even if these are seemingly at odds with one another. If I expect it of students, it must be a given for the educator as well.

As I explained in Chapters One and Two, Sandoval's differential consciousness and Anzaldúa's *mestiza* consciousness are conduits for extreme intellectual flexibility, where the knower can delink and link previously disparate knowledge to heighten new awareness and action. We get into ruts of knowing something very well, whether it is from experience or because we have studied it endlessly. We become incredibly well versed in advocating for issues we feel connected to; however, these tend to create blinders toward other, equally pertinent phenomena. I call this **conditional advocacy.** Making these interactions and occurrences explicit in the classroom is both necessary and a result of skilled negotiations in pedagogical spaces. It is keen attention to contradictions and asymmetries in power (not only between educator and student or among students but everywhere) that reclaims the potential for pedagogy to be a space where theory and practice become inseparable. No one is immune to or separated from perpetuating discriminatory or oppressive practices inside the classroom or out; therefore, it is critically important not to ignore one's responsibility in engaging **dangerous dialogues** or negotiating authority strategically in not silencing any one voice, not even your own, in order to expose the complexity of inequity and our complicity in it. Negotiations of power and authority are just some concepts feminist pedagogy makes vital to the learning process.

Consciousness raising became the trademark objective of the feminist movement in the 1970s. Many feminist classrooms rooted intellectual development, critique, and deconstruction in consciousness-raising strategies. The work that was more commonly done in community organizations or family homes moved partially into the academy, and soon classrooms took on the work of consciousness-raising groups. Classroom pedagogy accommodated the legitimacy of lived experience and personal nar-

Conditional advocacy

advocating for or on the basis of one category of identity at the expense of a more complex understanding of oppression, power, privilege, and lived experience

Dangerous dialogues

topics or issues considered controversial or historical events marginalized to maintain social control and complicity with dominant discourse

ratives in ways that problematized conventional curricular content and inquiry. Much work was done in related disciplines to pay closer attention to issues of gender, race, ethnicity, sexuality, class, culture, language, and so on as the landscape for pedagogical insight.

In the 1990s, the literature on feminist pedagogy grew as feminist educators grappled with how to hold true to politics, theory, and activism within the classroom and university space. Power again played an exaggerated role in the struggle for feminist pedagogy to exist and thrive in a highly bureaucratic institution. Power also manifested itself in the battles to define feminism, many times in erroneously singular ways. Feminist pedagogy hoped to make the learning experience more collaborative, personally meaningful, empowering, diverse, and challenging to the status quo. It needed to build literacy and foundational discourses, engaged pedagogy, and a rich politics of difference.

Some students came into feminist classrooms longing to be heard, while others expected to be silenced. Educators set up feminist classrooms with great hopes of institutional change, but what both groups found was a reappearance of social and individual pitfalls. The theoretical framework alone would neither resolve nor absolve the classroom dynamics from the difficulties of negotiating social, theoretical, political, and practical goals. Both students and teachers tried to shed the residue of past or concurrent educational experiences; nonetheless, competition, individualism, hierarchies, and essentialism were ever present. As a consequence, these dilemmas continue given the mutating, intricate structures of systemic power.

How, then, does one convince students traditionally displaced by theory or education to reclaim the intellectual endeavor of education? How does one convince students who have benefited from a traditional system of education that it does not serve all students equally? And how do we use these insights to forge pedagogies of coalition? It is important to demystify the notion that theory is hard and that we can or should talk only about our personal experience. Theory can be arduous yet instructional. Personal experience is undoubtedly educational yet incomplete given its self-referential scope. The historical distance from the 1960s and 1970s creates an assumption that all is well, that we have somehow dealt with gender discrimination, numbing critical questions, and views on how sexism continues to exist and mutate into various manifestations. Students are both deskilled and skilled because of the prevalence or familiarity of some notion of feminism in the public consciousness. Sound bites over the years have saturated some young students' minds, while others starve for more. The legacy of participatory education and consciousness raising is clear. The importance of struggle in both insight development and social change is pressing as we unfold the first decade of a new century.

Democratic education has always been at risk as ideological differences in the federal government shape its direction and existence. Regardless of its popularity or possibility, feminist pedagogy insists on the conditions of a democratic education, such as learning must involve freedom, social justice, participation, and community (even with its varying definitions). The major objective in using the framework of democratic education is to restructure the experience of pedagogy so that all its citizens feel mutually respected and the diversity of the group is retained and supported, at least in theory (feminist classrooms just like any other classroom sometimes do not feel particularly open or liberating). Yet at the heart of feminist intentions is the wish to establish an ethic of care in terms of how social projects are proposed and carried out. Many have grown skeptical of the ethic of care, as it tends to reinscribe women as inherently nurturing and to enact a superficial performance of care. Care is essential in creating sustainable social spaces for learning, but care must be politicized and held accountable to the interrelationship of overlapping modes of oppression. An ethic of care cannot be situated within discourses of civility or political correctness as these

are inclined to mask conflict and controversy. Care develops or grows out of participation, deliberation (communication and listening), and respect for both self and other in ways that may profoundly change private and public landscapes, micro and macro spaces.

The attempt at creating a democratic educational environment gives way to classroom dynamics that challenge the idea of just, participatory exchanges. There are times when democracy is counterproductive to the group moving in one direction or another. Pitfalls, limits, and parameters will always exist. The key is to articulate accurately what one stands for and how that is lived and to maneuver the twists and turns between ideas and actions. Feminist pedagogy is no different; as it borrows from a variety of pedagogies and philosophies it needs to keep rearticulating exactly how to carry out and modify its project, especially through recent popular avenues, service learning, and media studies.

Critical Post-structural Feminist Pedagogy

Feminist pedagogy is replete with hit and miss occasions, or *happenings,* if I can borrow a term from the art world, through which identities, ideas, and experiences clash or coalesce. These happenings, highly planned but spontaneous and flexible creative events, provide an excellent example where critical post-structural feminist pedagogy grapples with ambiguities and complex structures of knowing. Situated within hybridity, *mestiza-ness,* differential consciousness, and the trickster (discussed in Chapters One, Two, and Four), such pedagogy further deliberates and articulates, debunking binary thinking and practices. Instead of accepting static categories of identity politics, this type of pedagogy interrogates these constructions of positionality, while not discounting the important conduits of experience these have produced. Pedagogy sits at the intersection of understanding the systems of

oppression, one's location within these, and one's agency in negotiating such experiences.

Why critical *and* post-structural? Critical pedagogy (and theory) offers a distinct political analysis alerting us to the ways power operates in personal, cultural, historical, social, and educational systems. It focuses on how institutionalizations affect who we are and can be (in regards to race, gender, class, sexuality, language, culture, ability, religion, etc.), how justice and equality are defined, whose suffering counts, how we question dominant structures, and what role education plays in creating change. Critical pedagogy aims to develop and nurture critical consciousness to address larger political struggles and transformations in dealing with rampant oppressive social conditions. It works from Paulo Freire's critique on the banking concept of education to chart new pedagogical experiences, carefully mining popular culture for a wide range of learning possibilities. A transformative pedagogy is made possible by the close investigation of margins and center (that is, of power) and through the cultivation of critical consciousness, praxis, and engagement of the self as a public change agent. Post-structuralism as a social theoretical position offers deconstruction as a vital tool in peeling away layers of competing tensions and knowledge claims. It emphasizes the historical and cultural contingencies of all human experience (Kincheloe, 2004) and considers the struggle over language and meaning as a desirable process of identity construction. Orner (1992) explains:

> Instead of framing the slipperiness of identity as a problem to be solved or an obstacle to be avoided, feminist poststructuralists regard the inability to fix our identities and to be known through them in any definitive way as a powerful means through which we can "denaturalize" ourselves and embrace change. (p. 74)

Post-structuralism challenges the blatant acceptance of binaries as the only way to categorize or know the world. It offers language as a site of both constructed and contested meaning and a theoretical framework for teasing out the spaces between

either/or positions, and it provides a way to contend with the whole as an alternative to the juxtaposition of parts. Power is then understood as interrelated and interdependent, not as a singular hierarchal system but as a multidirectional and productive entity. So it is the conglomeration of critical pedagogy and theory, post-structuralism, and feminist pedagogy that creates hybrid happenings for knowledge production and praxis.

A critical post-structural feminist pedagogy, as a hybrid entity, developed for me through the years of teaching rigorous theoretical courses and pushing for more complexity in the ways we, as learners, came to know and act. I invited students to revel in the gaps of knowledge, to contemplate the unthinkable, and to enact these possibilities. There were many bumps along the way and many wrinkles to iron out over time, as I realized what I brought to the pedagogical table, so to speak.

A common objective for my courses is to figure out the relevance of theory in our everyday experience. The deciphering process is not easy as each student rethinks, resists, and constructs his or her understanding. As I have discovered throughout courses on feminist discourses in particular, there is a general assumption that feminist theory should be understandable by all and that it should always lead to action. So I ask, What is understandable? To whom? For whom? What is action? When does it happen? With whom? For whom? These questions seem imperative to accomplish what most students wish for, to unite theory and practice. I find the expectation that theory is automatically comprehensible of some concern, although not surprising. Theory for the most part is like clay or dough—it is supposed to be handled, manipulated, and transformed, not just agreed to or refuted. Theory, once understood and internalized, becomes inseparable from practice, yet the process of comprehension takes time. Room has to be given for the happenings mentioned earlier.

I agree with the assumption that all theory should be understandable, since for ideas to be productive and transformative, one must be able to comprehend them. No argument there. But what happens when theory is not readily understood? My distress is with what appears to be discouragement or frustration and little impetus to decipher, struggle with, or question that which at first seems alien. Unless we are willing, even through pain and confusion, to cross these unfamiliar borders, how is social change to occur? Sometimes this unwillingness is a result of few experiences in which students are repeatedly asked to analyze and decipher concepts or issues through conversation without expectation of "the" correct interpretation, where they are asked to listen and understand regardless of agreement. Seldom are students expected to sit within the spaces between the known and the to-be-known and actively to debunk the apparent absoluteness of binary oppositions or contradictions. We do not seem to be able to produce knowledge outside of the Hegelian dialectic. This is where post-structuralism and critical theory are particularly useful in helping students to explore nuance, complexity, sustainability, and interdependence in the production of knowledge.

Another important issue for a critical post-structural feminist pedagogy is the struggle over language and ideas, particularly those that challenge one's most familiar notions, and the will to figure something out that initially may seem quite difficult. It is this will and struggle that can subvert the stasis of inequity. As long as things continue to be unquestioned, change cannot occur. What may be understandable or knowable one day may change the next contingent on context or people involved. Not that everything is relative, as in a postmodern inferno, but meaning is interpretive and subject to shifts based on positionality (a combination of gender, race, age, class, ethnicity, culture, language, sexual orientation, faith system, etc.) and circumstance. The assumption that feminist theory should serve as a "how to" manual for empowerment demands that all feminist thinking speak to immediate gratification and that it dictate how to act and/or think

(somewhat contradictory to some of the tenets of feminist theory—self-discovery or actualization, empowerment, increased autonomy, and, yes, critical consciousness). This type of thinking does little to combat the consumerism created by patriarchy and capitalism. Thinking is a process. Transformation is a process. And these processes are circuitous, not linear or progressive in time and sequence; they take time, and sometimes painful insights ensue, creating small and drastic changes. The pluralism of feminist theories is flexible enough to embrace all sorts of writings and voices, both prescriptive and suggestive.

A constant request or demand expressed in classrooms is that what is read should be of direct use in one's living; if not, it is somehow not worth knowing. This is all well and good (and ultimately necessary), but, again, if the benefits are to materialize without any proactive engagement by the thinker or actor, then use or applicability will not occur. The burden of responsibility in merging thoughts or ideas and actions or practices is crucial and should rest with the reader or student (and here I include the educator as learner as well). I concur that many times we need concrete possibilities or examples of a different lived experience. On the other hand, these can lead to comfortable crutches, cause intellectual laziness, or perpetuate existing binaries. Within a classroom it is truly important to understand both expectations, to suit and challenge each in order to push what may or can be. To capitalize on the happenings, the pedagogical space must be a seedbed of creativity, feeding off its organic and dynamic structures.

I completely empathize with the insurgent desire to see a difference take place and also know the tempting inclination to fade into despair when one critique is read after another. Nevertheless, it is crucial to accept that changes obviously have been made (both good and bad) and will continue since the social and cultural environment is in constant flux. Our ability to engage the ambiguity of this flux better prepares us to accept and use any form

of agency available to us in the intersections of identities, theories, and experiences. The objectives of courses informed by feminist theories, women's and gender studies programs, queer studies programs, and others are not just to rid the world of the evils of patriarchy, as that may be a continuous (never-ending) project. Patriarchy, similar to any other system of power and ideology, shifts in its manifestations; therefore, the ways of resistance must mutate as well. Instead of getting depressed because inequality, sexism, racism, homophobia, xenophobia, and so on still exist, it seems more productive to understand these mechanisms as living entities and to confront and transform their negative and vicious repercussions. It is the actions we participate in every day and the intricacies of human relationships that map the critical ways individuals negotiate self and world. This is where theory is lived. I contend it is through these moments that transformative practice can take hold. I am more interested in how students live what they learn, read, and discuss. How does what learners read affect their thinking and feeling about others and about who they are or are made out to be in the multiple contexts they navigate on a daily basis? Perhaps it is stubbornness, but I resist the improbability of transformative knowledge leaking into action; if one truly reads for understanding, the words, ideas, emotions, and possibilities undoubtedly affect how one acts in the everyday toward oneself and others. Education does not happen only in the classroom or in the text; in fact, that is quite a privileged and elite space for learning. Education, learning, and transformation occur daily—in the supermarket, bank, social service office, driver's license office, playground, laundromat, bookstore, or health care provider's office, at a traffic light, ATM, mall, rally, or movie, on a street corner, bus, subway—as we interact with numerous people on any errand. These public spaces provide daily opportunities for theorizing and enacting theory into practice. Yet frequently we overlook them as we seek big overtures of drastic change. Here is where the worth of a critical post-structural femi-

nist education is lived and exercised for probably the majority of people. Unfortunately, these moments go unrecognized and ignored. We pass through happenings instead of partaking in them or creating them.

A critical post-structural feminist education may be just another academic exercise unless it plays its part in consciousness raising and developing a political critical awareness similar to traditional feminist pedagogy. It has been assumed that feminist pedagogy's audience is mostly women, but we know all too well this type of education is needed regardless of gender and because of gender. The work done in women's studies, gender studies, and gay, lesbian, and transgender studies is absolutely necessary. These programs in all their incarnations are crucial to the development of new discourses and possibilities for living, being, and thinking. As a society we have a difficult time evaluating programs, disciplines, and education in general. We search for quantifiable measures for qualitative phenomena. We look for numbers instead of living histories and narratives. We privilege abstract success through spoken promises and overlook the changes in voice, action, and relationships some of our students and teachers exhibit in both public and private spheres.

The importance of a critical post-structural feminist pedagogy is found in how feminism is defined, who has access to it, how students are to interact with it, and essentially how they live it, no matter who they are or where they come from, whether they claim to be "feminists" or not. We need to understand strategically and politically when it is necessary to use labels and when the actions speak louder than rhetoric. Placing a value judgment on either, seeing one as better or worse than the other, defeats a more richly nuanced understanding of how truly messy transformation and political action are. One of the positive elements of postmodernism is the acceptance of various or multiple interpretations. As a result, feminism can be a lot of things to many people; there need to be constants, whatever

they are, and these should lead to intellectual cultural work and political action. Traditional feminist tenets, "consciousness raising and political action," need to be defined and diversely interpreted for the highest level of impact on daily possibilities through intertextual polemics. A critical post-structural feminist pedagogy is indispensable, chiefly at a time when historical milestones fade in the distance and education becomes a standardized, fabricated disillusionment.

Structure of Curriculum

What does a critical post-structural feminist pedagogy look like? Many things, really. There is no set way or process for pedagogy; it is ever evolving, organic, and dynamic. I favor courses that foster large continuous conversations, and creating spaces for these interchanges is extremely important to all of our collective consciousness raising and theorizing. Creating these dialogues is never easy. I invite all participants to be present in whichever way is required for each day. In other words, although I prefer to hear what people are thinking regardless of whether they agree with each other, I do not force anyone to speak. I observe and listen to the silences carefully as these speak volumes about the intangibles in the space we inhabit. I continuously warn all of us about universalizing our perspectives, experiences, or desires. I ask many questions and request clarifications as we keep searching for new and different insights. Mostly through humor and sarcasm, I hold students accountable when discursive and experiential utterances or performances collide. We collapse time, turn it in on itself, and hold to cyclical curricular connections. We may be weeks away from a particular concept or reading, but if a student goes back to it, we all do for greater clarity or new questions. I also try to offer different evaluative experiences (assignments)—for example, creative projects that involve other ways of knowing and the use of symbolism as a language of difference (projects such as photoessays, zines, political posters,

pods, diptychs, self-designed aesthetic experiences, transnational postcards, and mailables). Students, even though they are quite anxious about these projects, end up creating extremely thought-provoking and enthralling pieces. My most basic criterion is that learning take place, that some movement or shift (decentering) occurs as a result of our collective pedagogical experience.

The courses are replete with various readings (maybe too many) that create dialogues with each other. In addition, songs, videos, magazines, zines, e-zines, spoken word performances, websites, and local events all become text for class discussion. In some courses I arrange the readings for the initial weeks of a semester and then ask students to choose the rest of what we will read together. They may do this in groups or individually, and they are responsible for getting us started in our discussions. At other times, I choose all the readings. For assignments I may offer different choices at midterm or final to open the space for ownership even further. The possibility always exists for students to tailor these even more to suit their particular research interests or social involvements. This is really not about what I do, but about what can be done, what we can all do regardless of our position in learning or teaching. I delve into my own pedagogy briefly only to provide some concrete vision of what critical post-structural learning has been in the classroom I share with countless other learners.

Service Learning/Experiential Education

Many regard service learning and experiential education as natural consequences of feminist theory and as practical enactments of feminism. The connection between feminist movements and activism set a historical precedent for the expectation that feminist ideas had to lead to social action and political engagement. Naples and Bojar (2002) believe that as women's studies programs became institutionalized, anxiety arose about compromising one's scholarship for political engagement, and risks for promotions

increased as a result of the politics of activism. Given these concerns, activist work has been sublimated into experiential education and service learning where connections between pedagogy and feminism can continue. So how are we defining service learning and experiential education?

Service learning is a form of education that requires active engagement in social issues through structured reflection, reciprocal relationships between the learner and the learned, critical questions, and problem solving of the project and its outcomes. Setting itself apart from community service or volunteering, service learning is multidirectional; it requires collaboration and partnerships to be respected and nurtured through the intentional engagement of the public in the institutional curriculum. It requires students to use what they know in ways that do not reinscribe current power hierarchies as they enter unknown territories and partner with others to accomplish mutually designed goals. In fact, for service learning to succeed the experience must suspend any assumption of absolute knowing, as most of the learning and activism happens in the co-construction of research, studying, learning, problem solving, and doing. Students must address real needs in the community through simultaneous active reflection and engagement with the political, cultural, and historical issues of the specific location or context. The most successful service learning experiences are those where participants have the courage to truly and critically question power, privilege, justice, and democracy around issues of race, class, gender, sexual orientation, ability, special needs, language, and a host of other social issues defining who we are in the larger civic context.

Experiential education values students' existing knowledge and actively incorporates it into the learning process. It privileges various ways of knowledge production and attempts to further a holistic educational experience. Carver (1996) states:

> Experiential education promotes the development
> of student agency, belonging and competence by

introducing resources and behaviors that allow for active learning, drawing on student experience, authenticity, and connecting lessons to the future in a learning environment that usually values caring, compassion, responsibility, accountability, individuality, creativity, and critical thinking. (p. 11)

Similar to service learning, experiential education requires active engagement and analysis, challenging students to take greater responsibility in their own learning and the impact such experiences have on others' learning. Such an education requires direct, authentic, active experience that develops future possibilities for community involvement and self-development. The student must be inquisitive and committed to participating in a profound meaning-making experience. Many believe experiential education can happen only outdoors, and although it is true that most of it does, many of the principles apply regardless of the setting. Students discover and experiment with who they are, who they thought they were, their capacities, and their potential. For many, the direct experience is the only way their thinking can be altered or shifted to understand what was previously unthinkable. So experiential education rests on the group experience yet focuses on what the individual learned. It may be coupled with a service learning project, but it is not dependent on that type of educational practice. Carver (1996) identified the ABC of experiential education as agency, belonging, and competence. Students gain personal agency, a sense of belonging and community, and competence in a variety of areas.

Both service learning and experiential education present rich methodologies for feminist pedagogy activism, yet neither offers any type of educational or theoretical panacea. It is the intention of this chapter not to universalize or standardize feminist pedagogy or activism but to suggest the complexities of current pedagogical quandaries as a source of possibility, of good risks to take in the enactment of theory and social change. Many times the desire for feminist service learning or experiential education grows out of a need to validate women's experiences in particular, as Nancy Naples discusses in her work. To some extent I agree, yet I would like to see a more engaged pedagogy address gender in general and not lock itself into women's experiences over the experience of others, as if power left some experiences untouched. Power affects everyone in both subtle and overt ways, and given larger historical patterns of inequity, minorities inclusive of either gender generally bear the larger brunt. There is neither disputing that nor masking it. What I offer is a delinking of feminist thinking and acting from a singular identity politics, not not naming these as feminist but underscoring these as such and making these pertinent to any one individual or group. This does not reject any historical grounding of the discourse; rather, it stresses its many origins and privileges a living, breathing historicity into the present and future.

A critical post-structural feminist pedagogy requires the rigorous engagement with service learning and experiential education to make the boundaries of learning and doing as porous as possible. One must consider institutional barriers only to understand further how to negotiate around these for greater possibilities of learning, not as cautions of what not to do. If we expect students to use pedagogy as an instrument for social change, we must be willing social agents ourselves, both in academic settings and in community spaces. This means revisiting the actual classroom space as a site for activism in all forms and resisting the divide between theory and practice. These divisions only perpetuate unproductive binaries and keep critical social change at bay, so that the only byproduct is the maintenance of the status quo.

Activism

I set activism apart from the previous categories to underscore the need to restructure our relationship to, and carrying out of, activism. Activism can be

folded into pedagogical contexts and can be lived on a daily basis regardless of context. Many look back to the 1960s and 1970s with some sense of nostalgia for its national waves of activism; seldom do we seem to recognize the activism that has continued through time, now and since the 1970s. Unfortunately, some of the critical minds of the past are locked into a certain definition of activism and tend to denounce the apathy of younger generations. The reality is that some people did get more comfortable with the beneficial consequences of past struggles, others were led to believe what the media communicated as they distanced themselves from the centers of action, and others remained skeptical of the comforts and made themselves available to mentor youth. One benefit that has continued to grow despite political pressure is the development of women's and gender studies, African American studies, ethnic studies, queer studies, interdisciplinary studies, cultural studies, and other programs of study focusing on cultivating a critical awareness around a plural politics of identity and power. These have been the seedbeds of new activism and thinking around issues of gender, race, ethnicity, class, culture, sexual orientation, religion, power, privilege, access, ecology, and aesthetics. The accessibility of technology has also expanded the ways in which people can connect and spread their ideas. Books such as *The Fire This Time: Young Activists and the New Feminism* edited by Vivien Labaton and Dawn Lundy Martin; *Grassroots: A Field Guide for Feminist Activism* by Jennifer Baumgardner and Amy Richards; and *Manifesta: Young Women, Feminism, and the Future* also by Baumgardner and Richards provide an incredible amount of information on what is happening at the beginning of the twenty-first century.

Just because universities and colleges house potentially transgressive programs does not mean that all sorts of institutionalized boundaries do not exist to keep difference confined to its own departments, programs, or token faculty, but again these hurdles are to be jumped over or gone under, not

left intact. The current political climate of thinking, acting, and imagining countercultural narratives is contentious in the wake of public pressure to stop the war in Iraq, reauthorize a defunct educational policy (No Child Left Behind, borrowed from a military tactic—leave no soldier behind), denial of same-sex marriages, deteriorating ecological sustainability, neglect of basic needs for individuals and families devastated by natural disasters, gouging of gas prices—the list goes on. Despite the concerted efforts to arrest resistance, it continues. No particular time in history (past and present) will provide more appropriate conditions than other times. The point of activism is to be active continuously, to have the courage to engage in critical questioning, and to have the strength to endure the alienation or rejection that may follow. Activism happens in all sorts of political climates; therefore, we should capitalize (to borrow a market term) on the spaces for feminist pedagogies to expand who is an activist and how activism is embodied.

How do we define activism? How is activism taught (if it can be taught) and how do we perpetuate it if indeed it is a desired outcome of a politically critical consciousness? Activism is an intentional action with specific goals or objectives toward accomplishing social or "political change work" (Walker, 1995). Ideally, activism is not acting for its own sake but acting that is fully informed by a critical and political consciousness with a direct purpose to create desired social change and positively impact people's lives. People are moved to act for various reasons; most often it is a direct experience with injustice, theirs or someone else's. Much debate exists about whether one can teach activism. Some say that since activism should surge from an internal motivation, it may be difficult to teach. Others say pedagogy can provide principles, skills, and catalysts, but not actual experiences. Instead of unequivocally saying one way or another, it seems that in developing activist pedagogy all of these perspectives need to be taken into consideration to craft successful experiences. There is much that can be done in the

classroom to foster compassion, connection, empowerment, creativity, and action. Courses on the history of activism, service learning, community involvement, grassroots organizing, nonprofit organizations, and many other things are necessary to build bridges from institutionalized spaces of learning to other, more amorphous ones and to solidify core tenets of feminist pedagogies.

Where to? What now? You tell me, what's the next source for civic engagement, for new directions, hopes, and collaborations? Thinking through what moves you is a first step, then research and learn who is doing what. A simple Google search will turn up thousands of possibilities. Local coffeehouses and organizations are also good sources of information; so are the courses that you are taking or the professors you know, non-mainstream magazines and zines. Last but not least, talk to the people you know or do not know yet to explore what are the current happenings.

GLOSSARY

Conditional advocacy—advocating for or on the basis of one category of identity at the expense of a more complex understanding of oppression, power, privilege, and lived experience

Dangerous dialogues—topics or issues considered controversial or historical events marginalized to maintain social control and complicity with dominant discourse

Intellectual flexibility—the ability to contend with various, sometimes opposing, ideas simultaneously for the sake of increasing agency and critical analysis

Notes

Chapter Two

1. A speech about women's suffrage given before the Chicago Political Equality League, 1897 (Spruill Wheeler, 1995, p. 191).

Chapter Three

1. A docent (the word being derived from the Latin word *docere,* meaning "to teach") is officially defined as a professor or university lecturer, but the term has been expanded to designate the corps of volunteer guides who staff many of the museums and other educational institutions in the United States. Docents are educators, trained to further the public's understanding of the cultural and historical collections of an institution (http://en.wikipedia.org/wiki/Docent).

2. First conceptualized in a sophomore seminar on the historical and social foundations of education, taught by Roy Carter, and as a consequence of our many conversations to help students develop solid methods of critical analysis. Students should be prepared for the side effects of engaging in critical analysis, such as rejection, alienation, and sacrifice.

3. I keep using both, "theorizing" and "action"—not for me, as I believe theorizing cannot exist without action and vice versa, but for those who may jump to conclusions; if I mention one, I do not mean the other. They are inseparable.

4. An important note: this simulation never equates to the lived reality of another person or group, so it must be entered tentatively and ever so suspicious of what one conjures. After all, it is a simulation with one or multiple authors, far removed from an autobiographical narrative.

5. For primary reads on "double consciousness," consult W. E. B. Du Bois and Franz Fanon. I borrow the term to highlight the various paradigms we often must balance, entertain, or negotiate if our thinking is slightly off from center.

6. I mentioned some of these in Chapter Two, but here are the texts I am thinking of specifically for this section: Valenti's *Full Frontal Feminism: A Young Woman's Guide to Why Feminism Matters*; Baumgardner and Richards's *Grassroots: A Field Guide for Feminist Activism* and *Manifesta: Young Women, Feminism, and the Future*; Labaton and Lundy Martin's *The Fire This Time: Young Activists and the New Feminism*; and a compilation of writings by young feminists: Hernandez and Rehman's *Colonize This! Young Women of Color on Today's Feminism*; Berger's *We Don't Need Another Wave: Dispatches from the Next Generation of Feminists*; Jervis and Zeisler's *Bitchfest: Ten Years of Cultural Criticism from the Pages of Bitch Magazine*; Moreno and Herrera Mulligan's *Border-Line Personalities: A New Generation of Latinas Dish on Sex, Sass, & Cultural Shifting*; Driver's *Queer Girls and Popular Culture: Reading, Resisting, and Creating Media*.

Chapter Four

1. Maxine Greene (1981) raises the necessity of "wideawakedness" (to be able to see and live with "eyes open") in using the humanities to create more meaning-making experiences in education. She states that "those with open eyes may at least be in a position to transform—or begin to transform—their lived worlds" (p. 398).

2. Paraphrased from Spinks (2001) Other key authors on tricksters are Paul Radin, Barbara Babcock-Abrahams, Marilyn Jurich, Christina O. Spiesel, Inna Semetsky, Robert Pelton, William Hynes, William Doty, Anne Deldon McNeely, Freda Edis, and others found in Spinks's book.

3. Maxine Greene (1981) discusses productive alienation brought about by engagement with the humanities and

various arts. I use productive alienation in course discussions to help students use the concepts that distance or marginalize them as productive sites for insight, turning the negative connotation of alienation into something useful.

4. This explanation arose from a class preparation session. My colleague Kathy Jamieson succinctly defined methodology for our graduate students. We team-taught a feminist research analysis course in the spring of 2007. The Harding 1987 reference comes from Sandra Harding's edited book *Feminism and Methodology: Social Science Issues.*

5. Nonsynchronicity is a way to rethink time and elements as not occurring together yet connected. The structure for connection is closer to multiple networks or rhizomes that still affect each other despite the potential distance between elements or events.

6. Deterritorializations and reterritorializations: Hicks (1991) uses these terms from the work of Deleuze and Guattari. Deterritorialization is the displacement from one's home or sense of home. It is a process of being plucked, disengaged, and decentered from the familiar. Reterritorialization is the process by which one reintegrates into a context that has been made familiar, a resettling of roots.

7. This is from Emily Hicks's *Border Writing* text (1991) where she illustrated what border writing is. Border theory investigates cultural, geographic, intellectual, political, and disciplinary borders, taking up postcolonialism and postmodernism as guides for interrogating these parameters and possibilities for crossing these borders. It often offers a language to discuss First World and Third World realities and unequal relations. Key authors are EmilyHicks, Jose David Saldivar, Gloria Anzaldúa, Norma Alarcón, and Americo Paredes.

Chapter Five

1. As the chapter unfolds, perhaps you will revisit Fisher's quote and see a need to substitute "women" for a term that highlights our attention to gender but does not reify the very binaries I recommend we decenter.

Resources
and References

Print Resources

Journals

Feminist and Gender Studies Journals

Affilia: Journal of Women and Social Work
http://www.sagepub.com/journal.aspx?pid=133

Camera Obscura
http://muse.jhu.edu/journals/camera_obscura

Chicana/Latina Studies: The Journal of Mujeres Activas en Letras y Cambio Social
http://malcs.net/issues.htm

Differences: A Journal of Cultural Studies
http://dukeupress.edu/differences

European Journal of Women's Studies
http://ejw.sagepub.com

Farzaneh (Iranian)
http://www.farzanehjournal.com/index.htm

Feminism & Nonviolence Studies
http://www.fnsa.org

Feminist Economics
http://www.feministeconomics.org

Feminist Review
http://www.feminist-review.com

Feminist Studies
http://www.feministstudies.org

Feminist Teacher (University of Wisconsin, Eau Claire)
http://www.uwec.edu/wmns/FeministTeacher

Frontiers: A Journal of Women's Studies
http://www.nebraskapress.unl.edu/journalinfo/17.html

Gender & Society
http://gas.sagepub.com

Hypatia: A Journal of Feminist Philosophy
http://www.iupress.indiana.edu/catalog/index.
php?cPath=519_580

Journal of Feminist Studies in Religion
http://www.hds.harvard.edu/jfsr

Journal of Lesbian Studies}
http://www.haworthpressinc.com/store/product.
asp?sku=J155

Journal of South Asia Women Studies
http://www.asiatica.org/jsaws

Michigan Feminist Studies
http://www.umich.edu/~mfsed

National NOW Times (National Organization for Women)
http://www.now.org/nnt/nntindex.html

NWSA Journal (National Women's Studies Association)
http://www.nwsaj.engl.iastate.edu

Signs
http://www.journals.uchicago.edu/Signs

Social Politics
http://sp.oxfordjournals.org

Tulsa Studies in Women's Literature
http://www.utulsa.edu/tswl

Woman's Art Journal
http://womansartjournal.org

Womanist Theory and Research
http://www.uga.edu/womanist

Women and Performance: A Journal of Feminist Theory
http://www.womenandperformance.org

Women's Review of Books
http://www.wcwonline.org/womensreview

Women's Studies Journal (New Zealand)
http://www.otago.ac.nz/press/journals/womensstudies/index.html

Women's Studies Quarterly
http://www.feministpress.org/wsq

Women's Studies: An Inter-disciplinary Journal
http://www.tandf.co.uk/journals/titles/00497878.html

Yale Journal of Law and Feminism{
"The *Yale Journal of Law and Feminism* is committed to publishing pieces about women's experiences, especially as they have been structured, affected, controlled, discussed, or ignored by the law. These experiences include the particular experiences of women of color and of lesbians."
http://www.yale.edu/lawnfem/law&fem.html

Queer Theory Journals

Angles: The Policy Journal of the Institute for Gay and Lesbian Strategic Studies
http://www.iglss.org/pubs/angles.html

Gay and Lesbian Review Worldwide
http://glreview.com/index.html

GLQ: Journal of Lesbian and Gay Studies
http://glq.dukejournals.org

Haworth Press
Haworth publishes several excellent journals of interest: *Harrington Gay Men's Fiction Quarterly, Harrington Lesbian Fiction Quarterly, Journal of Bisexuality, Journal of Gay & Lesbian Issues in Education, Journal of Gay & Lesbian Psychotherapy, Journal of Gay & Lesbian Social Services, Journal of Homosexuality,* and *Journal of Lesbian Studies.*

International Journal of Transgenderism
http://www.symposion.com/ijt/index.html

ONE National Gay & Lesbian Archives
http://www.onearchives.org

Nonprint Resources

General Information

EServer

"The EServer is a cooperative that has published writings in a wide range of arts and humanities fields, free of charge, to Internet readers since 1990." It is now based in the ISU English Department.
http://feminism.eserver.org

Feminista
"The online journal of feminist construction."
http://www.feminista.com

Feminist Majority Foundation
FMF "is a cutting edge organization dedicated to women's equality, reproductive health, and non-violence."
http://www.feminist.org/gateway

Gender Public Advocacy Coalition
"The Gender Public Advocacy Coalition (GenderPAC) works to end discrimination and violence caused by gender stereotypes by changing public attitudes, educating elected officials and expanding legal rights. GenderPAC also promotes understanding of the connection between discrimination based on gender stereotypes and sex, sexual orientation, age, race, class."
http://www.gpac.org

Gerritsen Collection—Women's History Online
"This online resource delivers two million page images exactly as they appeared in the original printed works. Users can trace the evolution of feminism within a single country, as well as the impact of one country's movement on those of the others."
http://gerritsen.chadwyck.com

Girls, Inc.
"Inspiring all girls to be strong, smart, and bold."
http://girlsinc.org

National Black Herstory Task Force
"The National Black Herstory Task Force, Inc. is a non-profit educational and cultural organization founded to provide vehicles to collect, research, authenticate, document, archive and celebrate the legacy and lives of women of African descent and their alliances."
http://blackherstory.org

National Organization for Women
"NOW is dedicated to making legal, political, social and economic change in our society in order to achieve our

goal, which is to eliminate sexism and end all
oppression."
http://www.now.org

National Women's Political Caucus
"The National Women's Political Caucus is a
multicultural, intergenerational, and multi-issue
grassroots organization dedicated to increasing women's
participation in the political process and creating a true
women's political power base to achieve equality for all
women. NWPC recruits, trains and supports pro-choice
women candidates for elected and appointed offices at
all levels of government regardless of party affiliation."
http://www.nwpc.org

National Women's Studies Association
"NWSA is committed to the development of scholarship
and research that incorporates disciplinary,
interdisciplinary, multidisciplinary, multicultural, and/or
global methods and perspectives to advance the study
and knowledge of all women and to create critical
dialogue on the production of knowledge about and
related to all women and on the application of such
knowledge to social and political practices and
processes."
http://www.nwsa.org

North American Women's Letters and Diaries
"North American Women's Letters and Diaries includes
the immediate experiences of 1,325 women and 150,000
pages of diaries and letters. Particular care has been
taken to index this material so that it can be searched
more thoroughly than ever before."
http://www.alexanderstreet2.com/NWLDlive

Sunshine for Women
[This is a topical collection of links to other sites.
http://www.pinn.net/~sunshine/main.html

Third Wave Foundation
"We strive to combat inequalities that we face as a result
of our age, gender, race, sexual orientation, economic
status or level of education. By empowering young
women, Third Wave is building a lasting foundation for
social activism around the country."
http://thirdwavefoundation.org

Women and Social Movements in the United States, 1600 to 2000
Provides more than 20,000 full-text documents, plus images, a chronology, and a dictionary.
http://alexanderstreet6.com/wasm

Women's Issues on the Internet

Facts Encyclopedia: Women's Issues
http://www.refdesk.com/women.html

Women's Studies/Women's Issues Resource Sites
This is "a selective, annotated, highly acclaimed listing of web sites containing resources and information about women's studies/women's issues, with an emphasis on sites of particular use to an academic women's studies program."
http://research.umbc.edu/~korenman/wmst/links.html

WWWomen.com!
A search directory for women online.
http://www.wwwomen.com

Feminism and Feminist Theory

Being Jane
"Being Jane provides access to advice, mentoring, support and a compendium of women-related information that leverages the experiences of women who have achieved non-traditionally female goals by actualizing their authentic beliefs and desires."
http://www.beingjane.com

Black American Feminisms
This is a "multidisciplinary subject bibliography of black American feminist writings."
http://www.library.ucsb.edu/subjects/blackfeminism

Feminist.com
"Feminist.com is a ten-year-old activist community and portal of resources and information that supports women's equality, justice, wellness and safety."
http://feminist.com

Feminist Theory
"This page lists links that are good resources or good starting points for research."
http://www.depts.drew.edu/wmst/StudentRes/www_femtheory.htm

Feminist Theory Website
> "The Feminist Theory Website has three parts: 1) various fields within feminist theory; 2) different national/ethnic feminisms; and 3) individual feminists. All of these parts are updated and expanded regularly."
> http://www.cddc.vt.edu/feminism/enin.html

Philosophy and Feminist Theory

Philosophy and Feminist Theory Sites
> http://www.library.wisc.edu/libraries/WomensStudies/philos.htm

Web Resources on Women
> http://www.bluegrass.kctcs.edu/LCC/WS/guide/phil.html

Women's Studies Resources: Feminist Theory
> http://bailiwick.lib.uiowa.edu/wstudies/theory.html

Queer Theory and Identity

Amnesty International Lesbian, Gay, Bisexual, and Transgender Network
> http://www.ai-lgbt.org

Bamboo Girl
> "To challenge racism, sexism, and homophobia as they relate to women of color, particularly those of Filipina, Asian Pacific Islander (API) and mixed Asian heritage."
> http://bamboogirl.com

Citizens Against Homophobia
> "Citizens Against Homophobia is a group that uses mass media campaigns to reduce homophobia."
> http://actwin.com/cahp

Erratic Impact
> Erratic Impact's Philosophy Research Base "attempts to aid both academic and general interest in all philosophical genres and their related fields." The LGBT Studies section "features hundreds of annotated links to Queer Theory and LGBT resources, designed to assist Lesbian, Gay, Bisexual and Transgendered people involved in academic study and philosophy research."
> http://www.erraticimpact.com/%7Elgbt

Gender Education and Advocacy
> "Gender Education and Advocacy (GEA) is a national organization focused on the needs, issues and concerns of gender variant people in human society."
> http://gender.org

GenderTalk
> "GenderTalk is the leading worldwide weekly radio program that talks about transgenderism in the first person. Each week we present news, information, and exciting new voices that challenge our traditional view of gender—and more."
> http://gendertalk.com

Human Rights Campaign
> http://www.hrc.org

International Lesbian and Gay Association
> http://www.ilga.org

Lesbian and Gay Equality Project
> http://www.equality.org.za

Les Voz
> A lesbian feminist site out of Mexico, entirely in Spanish.
> http://lesvoz.org.mx

National Gay and Lesbian Task Force
> "NGLTF is the national progressive organization working for the civil rights of gay, lesbian, bisexual and transgendered people, with the vision and commitment to building a powerful political movement."
> http://www.ngltf.org

PFLAG: Parents, Families and Friends of Lesbians and Gays
> "We, the parents, families and friends of lesbian, gay, bisexual and transgendered persons, celebrate diversity and envision a society that embraces everyone, including those of diverse sexual orientations and gender identities. Only with respect, dignity and equality for all will we reach our full potential as human beings, individually and collectively."
> http://pflag.org

Queer By Choice
> Queer theory links.
> http://www.queerbychoice.com/qtheorylinks.html

QueerTheory.com
> "QueerTheory.com provides you with the best online resources integrated with the best visual and textual resources in Queer Culture, Queer Theory, Queer Studies, Gender Studies and related fields."
> http://www.queertheory.com

Survivor Project
> "Survivor Project is a non-profit organization dedicated to addressing the needs of intersex and trans survivors of domestic and sexual violence through caring action, education and expanding access to resources and to opportunities for action."
> http://survivorproject.org

theory.org.uk
> Media/gender/identity resources.
> http://www.theory.org.uk/ctr-quee.htm

Transgender Forum
> Links and resources all around the country.
> http://www.transgender.org

Transgender Law and Policy Institute
> "We are a non-profit organization dedicated to engaging in effective advocacy for transgender people in our society. The TLPI brings experts and advocates together to work on law and policy initiatives designed to advance transgender equality."
> http://transgenderlaw.org

Transgender Legal Defense & Education Fund, Inc.
> "Transgender Legal Defense & Education Fund, Inc. is a national nonprofit civil rights organization committed to ending discrimination based upon gender identity and expression and to achieving equality for transgender people through public education, test-case litigation, direct legal services, community organizing and public policy efforts."
> http://transgenderlegal.org

Transsexual Women's Resources
> "Medical and Other Resources for Transsexual Women."
> http://annelawrence.com/twr

YouthResource
> "YouthResource, a Web site created by and for gay, lesbian, bisexual, transgender, and questioning (GLBTQ) young people 13 to 24 years old, takes a holistic approach to sexual health by offering support, community, resources, and peer-to-peer education about issues of concern to GLBTQ young people."
> http://youthresource.com

Zuna Institute
> "Zuna Institute is a National Advocacy Organization for Black Lesbians that was created to address the needs of black

lesbians in the areas of Health, Public Policy, Economic Development, and Education."
http://zunainstitute.org

Feminist, Pro-feminist, and Liberal Organizations

Association for Women in Psychology
"AWP is a not-for-profit scientific and educational organization committed to encouraging feminist psychological research, theory, and activism."
http://www.awpsych.org

Center for Women and Information Technology
The Center for Women and Information Technology is dedicated to encouraging global leadership and providing full access to technology. It seeks to enhance our understanding of the relationship between gender and Information Technology."
http://www.umbc.edu/cwit

Feminist Campus
All the tools you need to start your own feminist group.
http://feministcampus.org

Feminists for Life of America
A pro-life feminist organization.
http://feministsforlife.org

League of Women Voters
"The League of Women Voters, a nonpartisan political organization, has fought since 1920 to improve our systems of government and impact public policies through citizen education and advocacy."
http://www.lwv.org

NARAL Pro-Choice America
"NARAL has been the leading national advocate for personal privacy and a woman's right to choose."
http://naral.org

Planned Parenthood Federation of America
"Planned Parenthood health centers offer high-quality sexual and reproductive health care, including family planning, gynecological care, STI/STD testing and treatment, pregnancy testing, and abortion services."
http://www.plannedparenthood.org

WAMM: Women Against Military Madness
"WAMM is a nonviolent feminist organization that works in solidarity with others to create a system of social equal-

ity, self-determination and justice through education and empowerment of women. WAMM's purpose is to dismantle systems of militarism and global oppression."
http://worldwidewamm.org

Women's Sports Foundation
"The Women's Sports Foundation is a charitable educational organization dedicated to advancing the lives of girls and women through sports and physical activity."
http://www.womenssportsfoundation.org/cgi-bin/iowa/index.html

Law and Feminist Jurisprudence

American Bar Association Commission on Women in the Profession
http://www.abanet.org/women/home.html

American Civil Liberties Union
http://www.aclu.org

National Domestic Violence Organizations
http://www.usda.gov/da/shmd/nation.htm

National Women's Law Center (NWLC)
"Our mission is to protect and advance the progress of women and girls at work, in school, and in virtually every aspect of their lives."
http://www.nwlc.org

Ontario Women's Justice Network
"An online legal resource for women's organizations and individuals working on issues related to justice and violence against women and children."
http://www.owjn.org
U.S. Department of Justice Office on Violence Against Women
http://www.usdoj.gov/ovw

WomensLaw.org
"The mission of WomensLaw.org is to provide easy-to-understand legal information and resources to women living with or escaping domestic violence."
http://www.womenslaw.org

Media and e-Zines

3rd WWWave
A zine that reflects the "unique view of women's issues and feminism in the generation of women who came of age in the 80's. You'll find historical information that you might

not have known, discussion of politics, sexuality, daily life, sports and hobbies . . . and lots more!"
http://www.3rdwwwave.com

About-face
"About-face promotes positive self-esteem in girls and women of all ages, sizes, races and backgrounds through a spirited approach to media education, outreach and activism."
http://about-face.org

Adios Barbie
"AdiosBarbie.com is a one-stop body shop, where women and men of all cultures and sizes can learn about their bodies; feel proud and comfortable in their natural shapes, sizes, and colors; speak out against impossible beauty standards; and share their experiences."
http://adiosbarbie.com

Concerning Women
"A free information resource concerning the issues of today's women."
http://www.concerningwomen.com

Dads and Daughters
"Dads and Daughters is the national advocacy nonprofit group for fathers and daughters. DADs inspires fathers to actively and deeply engage in the lives of their daughters and galvanizes fathers and others to transform the pervasive cultural messages that devalue girls and women."
http://dadsanddaughters.org

Fat! So?
"For people who don't apologize for their size."
http://fatso.com

Grrrlzines.net
Links to all the zines you could want.
http://Grrrlzines.net

Guerrilla Girls
"We're a bunch of anonymous females who take the names of dead women artists as pseudonyms and appear in public wearing gorilla masks. In 18 years we have produced over 100 posters, stickers, books, printed projects, and actions that expose sexism and racism in politics, the art world, film and the culture at large. We use humor to convey information, provoke discussion, and show that feminists can be funny."
http://guerrillagirls.com

Listen Up! Youth Media Network
"Our mission at Listen Up! is to help youth be heard in the mass media, contributing to a culture of free speech and social responsibility. Listen Up! is a national Youth Media Network that helps youth producers and their adult mentors exchange work, share ideas and learn from one another."
http://listenup.org

Making Face, Making Soul: A Chicana Feminist homepage
"Making Face, Making Soul is a site by, for, and about Chicanas, meaning women of Mexican descent in the United States. This site contains a variety of resources ranging from short biographies of Chicanas, to Chicana poetry and literature, cultural resources, academic resources, otras chicanas on the 'net, and more."
http://chicanas.com

Media Education Foundation
"Guided by the belief that a media literate citizenry is essential to a vibrant democracy, the Media Education Foundation (MEF) produces and distributes video documentaries and other educational resources designed to challenge the accelerating threat to democracy posed by the commercial media system."
http://mediaed.org

Media Tank
"Media Tank is an innovative non-profit organization working to bring together media arts, education and activism to build broader awareness and support for media as a vital civic, cultural and communications resource."
http://mediatank.org

Media Watch
"Challenging racism, sexism, and violence in the media through education and action."
http://mediawatch.com

Moxie
"Moxie inspires women to live boldly, pursue adventures, take risks, and provide others with vibrant role models in the process."
http://moxiemag.com

Multiple Shades of You
E-zine and more for women of color.
http://msoyonline.com

Nervy Girl!
"The thinking woman's magazine."
http://nervygirlzine.com

Rockrgrl
"ROCKRGRL is a haven where women who play music can discuss our commonalities, our differences and our own unique perspective."
http://rockrgrl.com

Venus Zine
"Venus is the number one source for coverage of women in music, art, film, fashion, and D.I.Y. culture."
http://venuszine.com

Z magazine
"Z is an independent monthly magazine dedicated to resisting injustice, defending against repression, and creating liberty."
http://www.zmag.org/ZMagSite

Women's Health and Medicine

Abortion Clinics Online
"Abortion Clinics Online LLC (ACOL) is a paid directory service comprised of providers of abortion and other reproductive health care."
http://www.gynpages.com

American Public Health Association
http://www.apha.org

Black Women's Health Imperative
"Black Women's Health Imperative, the new name of the National Black Women's Health Project, is a leading African American health education, research, advocacy and leadership development institution. Founded in 1983 by health activist Byllye Y. Avery, it has been a pioneer in promoting the empowerment of African American women as educated health care consumers and a strong voice for the improved health status of African American women."
http://www.blackwomenshealth.org

Feminist.Com—General Women's Health
"Our web site is dedicated to promoting and sustaining women's well-being through the principles embodied in our motto: 'Awareness, Education, Activism and Empowerment.'"
http://www.feminist.com/resources/links/links_health.html

Feminist Women's Health Center—Cedar River Clinics in Washington State
http://www.fwhc.org

Johns Hopkins Bloomberg School of Public Health, Center for Communication Programs
http://www.jhuccp.org

Kaiser State Health Facts
"The Henry J. Kaiser Family Foundation is a non-profit, private operating foundation focusing on the major health care issues facing the nation . . . Through our policy research and communications programs, we work to provide reliable information in a health system in which the issues are increasingly complex and the nation faces difficult challenges and choices."
http://www.statehealthfacts.kff.org

National Asian Women's Health Organization
"Through its innovative programs, NAWHO is increasing knowledge of breast and cervical cancers, training violence prevention advocates, expanding access to immunizations, changing attitudes about reproductive health care, and breaking the stigma around depression and mental health."
http://nawho.org

National Women's Health Information Center, U.S. Department of Health and Human Services
http://www.4woman.gov

Native American Women's Health Education Resource Center
"In 1985, a group of Native Americans living on or near the Yankton Sioux Reservation in South Dakota formed the Native American Community Board (NACB) to address pertinent issues of health, education, land and water rights, and economic development of Native American people."
http://nativeshop.org/nawherc.html

Our Bodies, Ourselves
"Our Bodies, Ourselves (OBOS), also known as the Boston Women's Health Book Collective, empowers women with information about health, sexuality, and reproduction. We work in and for the public interest, promote equality between women and men, and build bridges among social justice movements."
http://www.ourbodiesourselves.org

Sakhi: Woman's Friend
"Sakhi for South Asian Women is a community-based organization in the New York metropolitan area committed to ending the exploitation and violence against women of South Asian origin. Recognizing oppression based on class,

immigration status, religion, and sexual orientation, we work to empower women, particularly survivors of domestic violence. Sakhi strives to create a voice and safe environment for all South Asian women through outreach, advocacy, leadership development, and organizing."
http://www.sakhi.com

U.S. Department of Health & Human Services, Specific Populations: Women's Health
http://www.hhs.gov/specificpopulations/index.shtml#women

U.S. National Library of Medicine
"The National Library of Medicine (NLM), on the campus of the National Institutes of Health in Bethesda, Maryland, is the world's largest medical library. The library collects materials and provides information and research services in all areas of biomedicine and health care."
http://www.nlm.nih.gov/nlmhome.html

Women's Health Matters, Sunnybrook and Women's College Health Sciences Center
http://www.womenshealthmatters.ca

Women's Studies Library and University Databases

Association of College & Research Libraries/American Library Association
Developed and maintained by the Women's Studies Section of the Association of College & Research Libraries. "The purpose of WSSLINKS is to provide access to a wide range of resources in support of Women's Studies."
http://libr.org/wss/WSSLinks/index.html

Five Colleges Archives Digital Access Project
This is "a digital archive of important historical resources in the Five College consortium. This Web site provides access to digitized versions of archival records and manuscript collections relating primarily to women's history—particularly women's education at the Five Colleges. Included among the collections are official college publications, letters, photographs, articles, oral histories, diaries, and more."
http://clio.fivecolleges.edu

Georgetown University Library's Guide to Research, Women's Studies
http://www.library.georgetown.edu/guides/women

Rutgers Libraries Resources on Women and Gender, Douglass Library
http://www.rci.rutgers.edu/~jsloan

Sallie Bingham Center for Women's History and Culture, Rare Book, Manuscript, and Special Collections Library, Duke University
http://scriptorium.lib.duke.edu/women/digital.html

University of Maryland, Women's Studies Database
http://www.mith2.umd.edu/WomensStudies

West Virginia University Center for Women's Studies, Eberly College of Arts and Sciences
http://www.as.wvu.edu/wvwmst

Women's Studies Librarian's Office, University of Wisconsin System
http://www.library.wisc.edu/libraries/WomensStudies/home.htm

Global Feminism (English language sites)

African Women and Child Feature Service
"The African Woman and Child Feature Service (AWC) is a Nairobi-based media organisation with an African regional outlook. AWC was established in March 1994 with the aim of mainstreaming gender in and through the media for development. Guided by the principle of equal development for women, men and children."
http://www.awcfs.org

African Women's Development and Communication Network
"The African Women's Development and Communication Network (FEMNET) was set up in 1988 to share information, experiences, ideas and strategies among African women's non-governmental organisations (NGOs) through communications, networking, training and advocacy so as to advance women's development, equality and other women's human rights in Africa."
http://www.femnet.or.ke

Amnesty International: Women's Human Rights
http://www.amnestyusa.org/women/index.do

Anarcho-feminist Group, Czech Republic
"Anarcho-feminist Group think that the deconstruction of the old structures and conventions (such as hindering gender roles, hierarchic relations, and alienation) has to take place together with the construction of new orders and relationships, which counts both for the whole society and the individuals."
http://www.fs8brezna.ecn.cz/files/english.html

Arab Women's Solidarity Association
"The Arab Women's Solidarity Association was established by a group of 120 women who agreed that the struggle for

the liberation of Arab people and freedom from economic, cultural and media domination cannot be separated from the liberation of Arab women."
http://www.awsa.net

Asian Women's Resource Exchange
AWORC "is an initiative geared towards developing cooperative approaches and partnerships in increasing access and exploring applications of new information and communication technologies for women's empowerment."
http://www.aworc.org

Association for Women in Development
"This international membership organization is committed to gender equality and a just and sustainable development process."
http://www.awid.org

Association of African Women Scholars
"Association of African Women Scholars (AAWS) is a worldwide organization dedicated to promoting and encouraging scholarship on African women in African Studies, forging intellectual links and networks with scholars, activists, students, and policy makers inside and outside Africa, and participating actively in continental and global debates on issues specifically relevant or related to African women."
http://www.iupui.edu/~aaws

Association of Albanian Girls and Women
"The Association of Albanian Girls and Women (AAGW), a non-profit humanitarian organization that empowers victims of human trafficking."
http://www.aagw.org

Bat Shalom of Jerusalem
"This feminist center for peace and social justice works toward a democratic and pluralistic society in Israel, where women will be of more influence."
http://www.batshalom.org

Caribbean Association for Feminist Research and Action
"CAFRA is a regional network of feminists, individual researchers, activists and women's organizations that define feminist politics as a matter of both consciousness and action. We are committed to understanding the relationship between the oppression of women and other forms of oppression in the society, and we are working actively for change."
http://www.cafra.org

Centre for Development and Population Activities
"Founded in 1975, CEDPA has provided services to millions of women through partnerships with 138 organizations in 40 countries. We begin with the individual to assure her access to high quality reproductive health and voluntary family planning. To sustain the services she needs and provide life-enriching skills, we strengthen community organizations that provide those choices and other vital support. Leaders of those groups, now more than 5,000 strong, form a powerful global CEDPA network. Together, we advocate at national and global levels to bring about lasting change for women."
http://www.cedpa.org

Centre for Leadership for Women
"The Australian virtual Centre for Leadership for Women aims to empower women to recognize their own potential to be leaders in a work and/or personal context, through experiencing an online environment that allows women: to learn from the experiences of leaders, both female and male; undertake self-evaluation; be able to express their personal and professional concerns and needs; and become informed about current leading issues and the individuals who are making it happen."
http://www.leadershipforwomen.com.au

Centre for Women, Family and Gender Studies, Moscow
"The Centre for Women, Family and Gender Studies was set up in June, 1993 as a non-governmental non-profit volunteer organization within the Moscow Youth Institute."
http://www.owl.ru/eng/women/aiwo/wom-cen.htm

Center for Women's Global Leadership
"The Global Center's programs promote the leadership of women and advance feminist perspectives in policy-making processes in local, national and international arenas. Since 1990, the Global Center has fostered women's leadership in the area of human rights through women's global leadership institutes, strategic planning activities, international mobilization campaigns, UN monitoring, global education endeavors, publications, and a resource center. The Global Center works from a human rights perspective with an emphasis on violence against women, sexual and reproductive health and socio-economic well-being."
http://www.cwgl.rutgers.edu

Center for Women's Studies in Education
"The Centre for Women's Studies in Education (CWSE) was established in July 1983 bringing together an existing core of feminist faculty, professional research staff (research

officers) and graduate students involved in the study of women and education."
http://www1.0ise.utoronto.ca/cwse

Coalition Against Trafficking in Women
"The Coalition Against Trafficking in Women (CATW) is a non-governmental organization that promotes women's human rights by working internationally to combat sexual exploitation in all its forms . . . CATW was the first international non-governmental organization to focus on human trafficking, especially sex trafficking of women and girls."
http://catwinternational.org

Committee for Asian Women
"CAW was set up as a joint ecumenical programme of CCA-URM and FABC-OHD which lay the groundwork for networking and publicizing the issues of women workers."
http://www.cawinfo.org

Equality Now
Equality Now is an "international human rights organization that works to end violence and discrimination against women and girls around the world. Issues of concern include rape, female genital mutilation, domestic violence, honor killings, trafficking in women and reproductive rights."
http://www.equalitynow.org

Face to Face International
"Face to Face is an international campaign to give voice to the millions of women denied basic human rights and freedoms. The goal of Face to Face is to increase global awareness that women's rights are human rights."
http://www.facetoface.org

Feminism in Hungary
The organization's aims are to promote the equality of men and women in Hungarian society and to fight against all kinds of discrimination, to increase awareness of women's issues and women's situation in Hungarian society, and to promote the participation of women in public life.
http://www.cddc.vt.edu/feminism/hun.html

Gaia International Women's Center
http://www.owl.ru/eng/women/aiwo/gaia.htm

Global Center for Women's Politics
"GLOW is an international forum for women from various cultural, national, and political perspectives. Their Web site features links to women's university programs, women's

activities and programs, and feminist bookstores and foundations."
http://www.glow-boell.de

Global List of Women's Organizations
http://www.distel.ca/womlist/womlist.html

Human Rights Watch
"Human Rights Watch is the largest human rights organization based in the United States. Human Rights Watch researchers conduct fact-finding investigations into human rights abuses in all regions of the world."
http://hrw.org

International Center for Research on Women
http://www.icrw.org

International Federation of University Women
"We are an international non-governmental organization (NGO) of over 160,000 women university graduates from seventy-four national federations and associations throughout the world. We are committed to education to influence and benefit society; the right of women and girls to education in order to reach their full potential; the recognition and protection of human rights; the promotion of peace, justice and equality; the development of international understanding, co-operation and friendship."
http://www.ifuw.org

International Gender Studies Resources
http://globetrotter.berkeley.edu/GlobalGender

International Women's Democracy Center
"The International Women's Democracy Center was established to strengthen women's global leadership through training, education, networking and research in all facets of democracy with a particular focus on increasing the participation of women in policy, politics and decision-making within their own governments."
http://www.iwdc.org

International Women's Media Foundation
"The IWMF's mission is to strengthen the role of women in the news media around the world, based on the belief that no press is truly free unless women share an equal voice." They raise awareness, create opportunities, and build networks. They have a successful program in Africa and leadership institutes yearly in the U.S."
http://www.iwmf.org/

International Women's Rights Action Watch
"The International Women's Rights Action Watch (IWRAW) was organized in 1985 at the World Conference on Women

in Nairobi, Kenya, to promote recognition of women's human rights under the Convention on the Elimination of All Forms of Discrimination against Women (the CEDAW Convention), a basic international human rights treaty. IWRAW now is the primary international nongovernmental organization that facilitates use of international human rights treaties to promote women's human rights and rights within families."

http://iwraw.igc.org

IranDokht

This site "utilizes more than 80 mostly Iranian female writers to contribute reports and articles on women's experiences and issues."

http://www.irandokht.com

KARAMAH

"KARAMAH: Muslim Women Lawyers for Human Rights is a charitable, educational organization which focuses upon the domestic and global issues of human rights for Muslims. KARAMAH stands committed to research, education, and advocacy work in matters pertaining to Muslim women and human rights in Islam, as well as civil rights and other related rights under the Constitution of the United States."

http://www.karamah.org/home.htm

LANIC, University of Texas Web Resources Guide for Latin American Women's Issues

http://lanic.utexas.edu/la/region/women

MADRE: Demanding Human Rights for Women and Families Around the World

"MADRE is an international women's human rights organization that works in partnership with women's community-based groups in conflict areas worldwide. Our programs address issues of sustainable development, community improvement and women's health; violence and war; discrimination and racism; self-determination and collective rights; women's leadership development; and human rights education."

http://www.madre.org

Mano River Women's Peace Network

"This bi-lingual site, published in French and English, highlights the work of this organization, a network of more than 100 civil society groups, particularly women's associations, located in Guinea, Sierra Leone and Liberia."

http://www.marwopnet.org

Maquila Solidarity Network

"The Maquila Solidarity Network (MSN) is a Canadian network promoting solidarity with groups in Mexico, Central America, and Asia organizing in maquiladora factories and export processing zones to improve conditions and win a living wage. In a global economy it is essential that groups in the North and South work together for employment with dignity, fair wages and working conditions, and healthy workplaces and communities."

http://maquilasolidarity.org

Moscow Center for Gender Studies

"MCGS formed in 1990 focuses on gender and research in Russia, gender theory has been recognized by the academic community and implemented into the curricula of many universities in Russia. First, MCGS pursued collective and individual studies using the gender approach and disseminated findings among researchers, teachers, political leaders and women's non-governmental organizations. Second, MCGS consolidated, expanded and improved its professional contacts with the academic and political institutions."

http://www.gender.ru/english

Muslim Women's League

"MWL is a nonprofit American Muslim organization working to implement the values of Islam and thereby reclaim the status of women as free, equal and vital contributors to society."

http://www.mwlusa.org

NANE Women's Rights Association, Hungary

"NANE is still the only NGO running a hotline for battered women and children in Hungary. Since our beginnings in 1994 the range of our activities has grown considerably. We have initiated amendments to laws and public administration reforms in areas where the current regulations do not guarantee equal protection under the law for victims of domestic violence."

http://www.nane.hu/english/index.html

Network of East/West Women, Poland

"Founded in 1991 NEWW is an international communication and resource network supporting dialogue, informational exchange, and activism among those concerned about the status of women in Central and Eastern Europe, the Newly Independent States, and the Russian Federation. NEWW coordinates research and advocacy that supports women's equality and full participation in all aspects of public and private life."

http://www.neww.org/en.php/home/index/0.html

Resources for and about Muslim Women
"Misinformation and misconception about Muslim women proliferate in the world today among non-Muslims and Muslims. I hope that instead of falling into the typical stereotypes and cultural innovation, the information here will pique your interest and help you to understand the true stance Islam takes on gender issues and the role of women."
http://www.jannah.org/sisters

Revolutionary Association of the Women of Afghanistan
"RAWA, the Revolutionary Association of the Women of Afghanistan, was established in Kabul, Afghanistan, in 1977 as an independent political/social organization of Afghan women fighting for human rights and for social justice in Afghanistan."
http://www.rawa.org

South Asian Women Network
South Asian Women Network "provides [a] forum for South Asian women who have immigrated to the West, and for those who live in South Asia. It provides practical news and resources on domestic violence, legal issues, and issues of marriage and divorce."
http://www.sawnet.org

STITCH
"STITCH is a network of women unionists, organizers, and activists that builds connections between Central American and US women organizing for economic justice."
http://www.stitchonline.org

United Nations Development Fund for Women
http://www.unifem.org

UNIFEM report on Colombia
http://www.womenwarpeace.org/colombia/colombia.htm

UNIFEM report on El Salvador
http://www.womenwarpeace.org/elsalvador/elsalvador.htm

UNIFEM report on Guatemala
http://www.womenwarpeace.org/guatemala/guatemala.htm

UNIFEM report on Haiti
http://www.womenwarpeace.org/haiti/haiti.htm

WINGS: Women's International News Gathering Service
"Raising women's voices through radio worldwide."
http://www.wings.org

Womankind Worldwide
"A UK charity dedicated to working internationally to raise the status of women."
http://www.womankind.org.uk

Women for Israel's Tomorrow (Women in Green)
http://www.womeningreen.org

Women for Women International
"Women for Women International was founded in 1993 to help women overcome the horrors of war and civil strife in ways that can help them rebuild their lives, families, and communities. Women for Women International's tiered program begins with direct financial and emotional support; fosters awareness and understanding of women's rights; offers vocational skills training; and provides access to income-generation support and microcredit loans that together can help women restart their lives in ways that are independent, productive, and secure."
http://www.womenforwomen.org

Women/Gender Studies Association of Countries in Transition
"Group formed to promote the research and professionalism of Women's Studies in former communist countries in Eastern Europe through an open exchange of ideas."
http://www.zenskestudie.edu.yu/wgsact/introduction.html

Women Living Under Muslim Laws
"Women Living Under Muslim Laws is an international solidarity network that provides information, support and a collective space for women whose lives are shaped, conditioned or governed by laws and customs said to derive from Islam."
http://wluml.org/english/index.shtml

Women of Pakistan
http://www.jazbah.org

Women's Edge Coalition
http://www.womensedge.org

Women's Freedom Forum, Inc.
"Women's Freedom Forum, Inc. is an independent organization advocating women's equality, legal and human rights, political participation and empowerment. It promotes women's health, children's rights, and equal job opportunities. Women's Freedom Forum aims to expose gender apartheid, fundamentalism, violence against women, misogyny, human trafficking, and child abuse and job discrimination.

Women's Freedom Forum is not affiliated with any government agency, political groups or parties."
http://www.womenfreedomforum.org

Women's Human Rights Net
WHRnet provides "comprehensive information and analysis on women's human rights and global issues."
http://www.whrnet.org

Women's Human Rights Resources
"The purpose of the Women's Human Rights Resources Web Site is to provide reliable and diverse information on international women's human rights via the Internet."
http://www.law-lib.utoronto.ca/diana

Women's International League for Peace and Freedom
"WILPF was the first international peace organization founded by women in the world organized in Europe in 1915. It was started at the Hague during World War I, and its effect on public policy over the past 80 years has been enormous. In our society, where the root causes of constant international and domestic crises are hard to grasp, WILPF offers analysis and a quick way to join with others in taking action."
http://www.wilpf.org

WomenWatch
United Nations Inter-Agency Network on Women and Gender Equality
http://www.un.org/womenwatch

Women @ Latin American Information Agency
http://alainet.org/mujeres

References

Adams, R., & Savran, D. (Eds.). (2002). *The masculinities studies reader*. Oxford: Blackwell Publishing.

Ainger, K. (2002). Mujeres Creando: Bolivian anarcha-feminist street activists. In Dark Star Collective (Ed.), *Quiet rumours: An anarcha-feminist reader*. Oakland, CA: AK Press.{AQ: Page numbers?} don't have it with me.

Alderson, D., & Anderson, L. R. (2000). *Territories of desire in queer culture: Refiguring contemporary boundaries*. Manchester, UK: Manchester University Press.

Andersson, M. (2000). The situated politics of recognition, ethnic minority, youth and identity work. London: Goldsmiths College, University of London. Available at http://www.goldsmiths.ac.uk/cucr/pdf/andersson.pdf.

Anzaldúa, G. (1999). *Borderlands, la frontera: The new mestiza* (2nd ed.). San Francisco: Aunt Lute.

Anzaldúa, G. (2002). Now let us shift . . . the path of *conocimiento* . . . inner work, public acts. In G. Anzaldua & A. Keating (Eds.), *This bridge we call home: Radical visions for transformation* (pp. 540–592). New York: Taylor & Francis.

Bardran, M. (2006). Islamic feminism revisited. Available at http://www.countercurrents.org/gen-badran100206.htm.

Barnes, S. L. (2007). Black American feminisms: A multidisciplinary bibliography. Available at http://www.library.ucsb.edu/subjects/blackfeminism/introduction.html.

Beasley, C. (1999). *What is feminism? An introduction to feminist theory.* London: Sage Publications.

Brayton, J. (1997). What makes feminist research feminist? The structure of feminist research within the social sciences. Available at http://www.unb.ca/web/PAR-L/win/feminmethod.htm.

Britzman, D. P. (1998). Is there a queer pedagogy? Or, stop reading straight. In W. Pinar (Ed.), *Curriculum: Toward new identities.* New York: Routledge.

Bunch, C. (1993). Lesbians in revolt. In A. M. Jaggar & P. S. Rothenberg (Eds.), *Feminist frameworks: Alternative theoretical accounts of the relations between women and men* (3rd ed.). Boston: McGraw-Hill. {AQ: Page numbers?} don't have it with me

Carver R. (1996). Theory for practice: A framework for thinking about experiential education. *Journal of Experiential Education, 19*(1), 9–13.

Connell, R. W. (1995). *Masculinities.* Berkeley: University of California Press.

Davis, B., Sumara, D., & Luce-Kapler, R. (2000). *Engaging minds: Learning and teaching in a complex world.* Mahwah, NJ: Lawrence Erlbaum Associates.

Eaton, H. (2003). Can ecofeminism withstand corporate globalization? In H. Eaton & L. A. Lorentzen (Eds.), *Ecofeminism and globalization: Exploring culture, context, and religion.* Lanham, MD: Rowman & Littlefield.{AQ: Page numbers?} don't have it with me

Esteban Muñoz, J. (1999). *Disidentifications: Queers of color and the performance of politics.* Minneapolis: University of Minnesota Press.

Fisher, B. M. (2001). *No angel in the classroom: Teaching through feminist discourse.* Lanham, MD: Rowman & Littlefield.

Frye, M. (1993). The possibility of feminist theory. In A. M. Jaggar & P. S. Rothenberg (Eds.), *Feminist frameworks: Alternative theoretical accounts of the relations between women and men* (3rd ed). Boston: McGraw-Hill. {AQ: Page numbers?} don't have it with me

Goldman, E. (1911). Woman suffrage. In *Anarchism and other essays* (2nd revised ed.) (pp. 201–215). New York and London: Mother Earth Publishing Association. Available at http://dwardmac.pitzer.edu/Anarchist_Archives/goldman/aando/suffrage.html.

Grant, J. (1993). *Fundamental feminism: Contesting the core concepts of feminist theory.* New York: Routledge.

Green, E., & Adam, A. (Eds.). (2001). *Virtual gender: Technology, consumption and identity.* London: Routledge.

Greene, M. (1981). The humanities and emancipatory possibilities. *Journal of Education, 163*(4).{AQ: page numbers?} don't have it with me

Grewal, I., & Kaplan, C. (2000). Postcolonial studies and transnational feminist practices. *Jouvert: Journal of Postcolonial Studies, 5*(1). Available at http://social.chass.ncsu.edu/jouvert/v5i1/grewal.htm.

Haraway, D. J. ([1985] 1991). A cyborg manifesto: Science, technology, and socialist-feminism in the late twentieth century. In *Simians, cyborgs and women: The reinvention of nature* (pp. 149–181). New York: Routledge.

Hartman, G. H. (1993). Public memory and modern experience. *Yale Journal of Criticism, 6*(2), 239–247.

Heywood, L., & Drake, J. (Eds.). (1997). *Third wave agenda: Being feminist, doing feminism.* Minneapolis: University of Minnesota Press.

Hicks, D. E. (1991). *Border writing: The multidimensional text.* Minneapolis: University of Minnesota Press.

hooks, b. (1984). *Feminist theory: From margin to center.* Cambridge, MA: South End Press.

Hymowitz, C., & Weissman, M. (1978). *A history of women in America.* New York: Bantam.

Jaggar, A. (1983). Feminist politics and epistemology: Justifying feminist theory. In *Feminist politics and human nature.*

Brighton, UK: Harvester.{AQ: Page numbers?} don't have it with me

Jagose, A. (1996). *Queer theory: An introduction.* New York: New York University Press.

James, J. (2000). Radicalizing feminism. In J. James & T. D. Sharpley-Whiting (Eds.), *The black feminist reader.* Malden, MA: Blackwell. {AQ: Page numbers?} don't have it with me

Jones, A. (Ed.). (2003). *The feminism and visual culture reader.* New York: Routledge.

Kazmierczak, E. T. (2001). Why do we want tricksters? In C. W. Spinks (Ed.), *Dance of differentiation: Trickster and ambivalence.* Madison, WI: Atwood Publishing. {AQ: Page numbers?} don't have it with me

Kessler, S. J., & McKenna, W. (1978). *Gender: An ethnomethodological approach.* Chicago, IL: University of Chicago Press.

Kincheloe, J. L. (2004). *Critical pedagogy: A primer.* New York: Peter Lang.

Kornbluh, J. (n.d.). Bread and roses: The 1912 Lawrence textile strike. Available at http://www.lucyparsonsproject.org/iww/kornbluh_bread_roses.html.

Lincoln, Y. S., & Guba, E. G. (2000). Paradigmatic controversies, contradictions, and emerging confluences. In N. K. Denzin & Y. S. Lincoln (Eds.), *Handbook of qualitative research* (2nd ed.) (pp. 163–188). Thousand Oaks, CA: Sage.

Lorber, J. (2005). *Gender inequality: Feminist theories and politics* (3rd ed.). Los Angeles: Roxbury Publishing Company.

Lugg, C. (2007). Gender, sexual orientation and a new politics of education? In D. Carlson & C. P. Gause (Eds.), *Keeping the promise: Essays on leadership, democracy, and education.* New York: Peter Lang.{AQ: Page numbers?} don't have it with me

MacInnes, J. (1998). *The end of masculinity: The confusion of sexual genesis and sexual difference in modern society.* Philadelphia, PA: Open University Press.

Marcuse, H. (1978). *The aesthetic dimension.* Boston: Beacon Press.

Matthews, J. J. (1985). Good and mad women: The historical construction of feminity in twentieth century Australia. New York: Australia.

Messner, M. A. (2000). *Politics of masculinities: Men in movements.* New York: AltaMira Press.

Mirande, A. (1997). *Hombres y machos: Masculinities and Latino culture.* Boulder, CO: Westview.

Mohanty, C. T. (2003). *Feminism without borders: Decolonizing theory, practicing solidarity.* Durham, NC: Duke University Press.

Morris, M. (1998). Unresting the curriculum: Queer projects, queer imaginings. In W. Pinar (Ed.)., *Queer theory in education.* Mahwah, NJ: Earlbaum.

Mother Jones (n.d.). The autobiography of Mother Jones. Available at http://www.angelfire.com/nj3/RonMBaseman/mojones1.htm.

Namaste, V. K. (2000). *Invisible lives: The erasure of transsexual and transgendered people.* Chicago, IL: University of Chicago Press.

Naples, N., & Bojar, K. (2002). *Teaching feminist activism: Strategies from the field.* New York: Routledge.

Nisbet, R. (1976). *Sociology as an art form.* London: Oxford University Press.

An Operative. (1845a). Factory life as it is. *Factory Tracts, 1.* Available at http://historymatters.gmu.edu/d/6217.

An Operative. (1845b). Some of the beauties of our factory system—Otherwise, Lowell Slavery. *Factory Tracts, 1.* Available at http://historymatters.gmu.edu/d/6217.

Orner, M. (1992). Interrupting calls for student voice in "liberatory" education: A feminist poststructuralist perspective. In C. Luke & J. Gore (Eds.), *Feminism and critical pedagogy* (pp. 74–78). New York: Routledge.

Pilcher, J., & Whelehan, I. (2004). *50 key concepts in gender studies.* Thousand Oaks, CA: Sage.

Richardson, L. (2000). New writing practices in qualitative research. *Sociology of Sport Journal, 17,* 5–20.

Sandoval, C. (1991). U.S. third world feminism: The theory and method of oppositional consciousness in the postmodern world. *Genders, 10* (Spring), 1–24.

Sandoval, C. (1995). New sciences: Cyborg feminism and the methodology of the oppressed. In C. Hables Gray's *The Cyborg Handbook* (Ed.)., New York: Routledge.

Schulz, D. (2001). Speaking to survival. *Awakened Woman: The Journal of Women's Spirituality.* Spring/Summer. Available at http://www.awakenedwoman.com/native_women.htm.

Shah, S. (1997). *Dragon ladies: Asian American feminists breathe fire.* Cambridge, MA: South End Press.

Shlasko, G. D. (2005). Queer (v.) pedagogy. *Equity & Excellence in Education, 38,* 123–134.

Shohat, E. (1999). *Talking visions: Multicultural feminism in a transnational age.* Cambridge, MA: MIT.

Spinks, C. W. (2001). Trickster and duality. In C. W. Spinks (Ed.), *Dance of differentiation: Trickster and ambivalence.* Madison, WI: Atwood Publishing.

Spruill Wheeler, M. (Ed.). (1995). *One woman, one vote: Rediscovering the woman suffrage movement.* Troutdale, OR: NewSage Press.

Stryker, S., & Whittle, S. (Eds.). (2006). *The transgender reader.* New York: Routledge.

Villaverde, L. E. (2006). The aesthetic dimension of youth culture education. In S. Steinberg, P. Parmar, & B. Richard (Eds.), *Contemporary youth culture: An international encyclopedia,* Volume 2. Westport, CT: Greenwood Press.

Walker, R. (1995). To be real: Telling the truth and changing the face of feminism. New York: Anchor Books.

Wiegman, R. (2002). Unmaking: Men and masculinity in feminist theory. In J. Kegan (Ed.), *Masculinity studies and feminist theory: New directions.* New York: Columbia University Press.

Wittig, M. (1980). *The straight mind: And other essays.* Boston: Beacon Press.

Peter Lang PRIMERS

in Education

Peter Lang Primers are designed to provide a brief and concise introduction or supplement to specific topics in education. Although sophisticated in content, these primers are written in an accessible style, making them perfect for undergraduate and graduate classroom use. Each volume includes a glossary of key terms and a References and Resources section.

Other published and forthcoming volumes cover such topics as:

- Standards
- Popular Culture
- Critical Pedagogy
- Literacy
- Higher Education
- John Dewey
- Feminist Theory and Education

- Studying Urban Youth Culture
- Multiculturalism through Postformalism
- Creative Problem Solving
- Teaching the Holocaust
- Piaget and Education
- Deleuze and Education
- Foucault and Education

Look for more Peter Lang Primers to be published soon. To order other volumes, please contact our Customer Service Department:

800-770-LANG (within the US)
212-647-7706 (outside the US)
212-647-7707 (fax)

To find out more about this and other Peter Lang book series, or to browse a full list of education titles, please visit our website:
www.peterlang.com